WHEN *the*
ROCKS
SING

A STORY *of* LOVE, LOSS, *&*
LEARNING *to* LIVE AGAIN

Marv Weidner &
Carol GoldfainDavis MA, LPC

Ballast Books, LLC
Washington, DC
www.ballastbooks.com

ISBN 978-1-955026-32-1

Library of Congress Control Number has been applied for

Printed in Hong Kong

Published by Ballast Books
www.ballastbooks.com

For more information, bulk orders, appearances or speaking requests,
please email info@ballastbooks.com

MARV

*This is dedicated to Marty's Indomitable Spirit
And our children and grandchildren Emily, Chris,
Seth, Isabel, Sophia, Ava Grace, Malcolm*

CAROL

*This is dedicated to so many precious, grieving souls
who over the years have taught me that love truly lasts forever,
to my family who patiently endured my writing absences,
and to Marv, who continues to show us that
resilience exists and empowers.*

TABLE OF CONTENTS

Author's Note

Welcome. This is a story about two people very much in love. Marty and I built a life together. We shared everything by keeping our hearts open to each other. Our life together was interrupted by a cancer diagnosis that ultimately took Marty's life. Please join me as I tell this story of loss, grief and the ways in which, with Marty's help, I was able to love life and move forward again.

Marty and I met each other in 1998 as work colleagues. Our relationship grew into a friendship, then lovers, and then spouses. From the time we were married in 2002, we created a world unto ourselves—as romantic partners, business partners and co-parents—and were each other's best friend. Our relationship was always our #1 priority.

In September 2016, Marty was diagnosed with stage-4 lung cancer. We fought it together and we fought with all our might. But ultimately Marty passed away, freeing herself from the cancer on Independence Day on July 4, 2017, only nine months after the diagnosis. The book follows us through the cancer journey, how we kept our love strong and stayed present on every one of those precious days.

I want you to hear about Marty's incredible strength as she lived each day as fully as possible and faced death with uncommon courage. I also want you to see how I experienced the great waves of grief that followed her passing and what I did to survive it and grow.

My co-author, Carol GoldfainDavis (M.A. LPC, CAGCS, NAMAS-II, Hospice Social Worker, Individual and Family Counselor) was Marty's and my grief counselor. We have collaborated in each chapter—her comments following my story-- to create a unique combination of personal experience and clinical insights into grief.

Our focus is on how to tap into and rebuild the resiliency it takes to survive and thrive after a great loss. Our two voices provide a unique perspective on an experience that is universal to us all: the loss of a loved one.

Carol, who practices in the Gunnison Valley on the Western Slope of Colorado, shares her deep wisdom earned from many years as a grief counselor, as well as insights from the literature she has studied about grief and resiliency. Her work and her voice speak not only to those who have experienced loss but also to the friends, family, counselors, spiritual advisers, social workers, hospice nurses and others who provide support to those experiencing loss.

Loss is an inherent, integral part of life. Love and loss are inseparable. If we live long enough, we will all lose someone we love. In the same way that I believe grief is best handled by engaging it head-on, I have tried to share my journey as honestly and straightforwardly as I can. I hope that you will identify with my experience, and we can go through this together. More than anything I want you to know you are not alone.

Although many of the insights come from the depths of grief, this is a book about hope, about finding the resiliency within you to move forward to rebuild your life after losing a loved one. My stories track Marty's cancer journey, my grief and what I discovered along the way about life, love, loss, grief and living with an open heart.

I tried to write my stories with a no-holds-barred honesty. Only by being completely honest can we face the hard parts of life, rebuild the resiliency that will take us forward and help us fully love and embrace life once again. Grief resulting from the loss of a loved one can overwhelm us for a time, it will become part of us always, but it does not determine our future. We can choose to be happy, choose our purpose and how we will live each day.

The title of the book, "When the Rocks Sing", comes from the moment in early 2018, six months after Marty passed, when I found that I was still in love with life. The disc-shaped rocks on the beach at Greymouth, New Zealand chatter against each other as the waves wash over them on the way back out to sea. Their song is quiet and has its own unique rhythm. On a day at a beach halfway around the world from my home, I was able to quiet the chaos that had occupied my mind and soothe the pain in my heart so I could hear the rocks sing. In that moment I once again felt the joy of being alive.

Then and now, I seek to embrace the impermanence of life in a way that creates both a sense of urgency and freedom to live in the present moment. My heart and thoughts are with you, as you, too, will arrive at a moment in your grief when your heart and mind can be still in the moment and you can feel the joy of being alive.

In writing this book, Carol and I have tried to illuminate the organic nature of grief that creates a unique experience in each individual's life. Each of us has our own perspective on loss and we experience grief in our own way. Past theories sought to make sense of the grief process by attributing structure to it, for example as stages. However, one size does not fit everyone. In fact, there is no "structure" at all, but rather a continuous process of feelings, memories, questions, hope, discovery and growth. Nor is there a timeline that fits any two people's experiences.

Without imposing an artificial structure or timeline for the grief we live through and with, Carol and I have written a down-to-earth, practical and non-technical guide for surviving the loss of a loved one and, with resiliency as the bedrock, moving forward with life.

We are very aware that the book is becoming available at a time when the loss of loved ones has impacted nearly everyone. The pandemic has touched the families, friends and communities of more than 1,000,000 people who have died from COVID 19 in the US and more than 6 million globally, at this writing. Our hearts are with those who have lost loved ones.

This I know:
Love cannot
    Defeat Death, But
Death cannot
    Defeat Love.

Marv Weidner, January, 2021

CHAPTER 1

———

MY STORY

This is a love story about two people. You may know people just like them, or you might be just like them. It is the story of how these two people loved each other with all their hearts and together faced the hardest thing they had ever faced: a cancer diagnosis with a terminal prognosis. Join Marty (my wife) and Marv (that's me) in our race to savor each day and all it had to offer. Come along on our journey as we faced the hard stuff head-on, while keeping love and joy alive.

Walk with me while I share stories, experiences and insights from my own tremendous loss and deeply-felt grief process. Learn what I have learned, some of which is conventional but some that is decidedly unconventional—and all of which is, hopefully, inspirational. Come along to explore your own resiliency to recover from loss and what it means to live a full life while staying aware of the impermanence of all that we know.

In each chapter, our deeply wise grief counselor, Carol Gold-fainDavis, tells us what is most important to know about each challenge we face during and after a loss. From her years as a grief counselor, she offers practical wisdom for how we can build, access and restore the resiliency we tap into each time we experience a loss. She gives us guidance on how we can move from loss through grief and how to recover to fully embrace life once again.

WHAT DID I BRING?

What did I bring to the experience of Marty's cancer and death? I brought an open heart wildly in love with Marty. We had been together for eighteen years when we got the phone call telling us that she had cancer, and that it had metastasized in her brain and bones. We had lived together with a commitment to share everything, hold nothing back, face reality no matter what it was. We built a successful business, parented children from previous marriages, and practiced Zen meditation and mindfulness.

I came from a normal, albeit dysfunctional, family. My home was in a rural part of Iowa, just outside a small county seat town in the middle of cornfields. Both of my sets of grandparents, and most of their friends, were farmers. My parents were typical depression-era children who grew up with a sense of scarcity and an overwhelming, primary focus on economic security.

I remember sitting in my chair at the lunch table and my Mom telling me how much money a particular family had. In my own childlike way—I was about seven years old at the time—I asked why that was important. She replied that the amount in your bank account was what you are worth. I asked if I was only worth $35 because that is all I had in my account. She said, 'Yes.'

I was not like my family, nor was I liked by them. Even as a very young child I believed in the common humanity of everyone and rejected my family's prejudices toward people who were different from us. The day I started kindergarten, I went to the water fountain to get a drink. My Mom told me not to touch it with my lips because an 'Indian kid' may have drunk from it. I knew all the way through my being that she was wrong to think that way.

I grew up with Native American kids and my best friend in junior and senior high was from the only African American family in the county. On trips, my family would find me talking with strangers no matter what they looked like. I loved people as a child. On a trip to New York City when I was four years old, my folks lost track of me in the hotel lobby. They found me speaking with a family from Spain. The family did not speak English and, of course, I didn't speak Spanish. That happened often with me, and I could see that it embarrassed my family.

As a child, I overheard family members talking about me in terms that were so critical, I wondered if they might send me away. I was an outlier, to say the least, but I knew all along that the way I felt about people was right.

Overall, though, I had a decent childhood. I played outside every day. In the summers, I was out the door shortly after sunrise and back again after sunset, coming in and out of the screen door for meals. During high school, I played sports, took home 12 varsity letters, earned gas money working on farms and dated farmers' daughters.

Growing up in small-town Iowa was a great experience. I hunted and fished, baled hay, and had great friendships. In that stable, rural setting I was witness to the cycles of life in the annual planting and harvesting of the crops, in livestock raised and sent on to become a food source, and in the lives of people, too. The cycle of life and the impermanence of life was everywhere and obvious. When I was in the second grade, two of my classmates, twins, were killed in a tractor accident. My grandparents passed away and I heard about the murders of Bobby and John F. Kennedy, Malcolm X and Martin Luther King.

There were other hard parts. My brother, who was five years

older than me, beat me up roughly once a week from the time I was five. I guess that is why I grew up fighting bullies. If there was someone bullying another kid of lesser strength, I intervened with fists flying. I was a tough kid and never lost those fights. As a consequence, I spent a good bit of time in the principal's office at school. When I was fifteen and finally able to stand up to my brother, I stopped his bullying with a well-landed punch on his nose. I really hated bullies, and still do.

All of this led to a kind of inner strength and resiliency in the face of being ostracized and rejected. Somehow, I never saw myself as a victim, and I think that eliminated what could have been a serious barrier to inner strength.

I'd had failed marriages due to a lack of self-awareness, but I raised two wonderful children under those circumstances, had a successful 20-year career in government, and managed to earn an undergraduate degree in political science and economics and a graduate degree in theology. By the time Marty and I met, I had started practicing Zen meditation and done a lot of work on myself. I was ready for a successful relationship with an incredibly loving, intellectually and emotionally intelligent, wise and beautiful woman.

What I wasn't prepared for was Marty dying from cancer. Cancer was the one bully that I could not defeat.

It was these notions—our common humanity, the impermanence of all living things, the urgency to live life fully and to face death as part of life—that had built my internal reservoir of resiliency to face Marty's cancer and her certain death. Being loved so well by Marty Weidner for 19 years kept that reservoir full and overflowing.

We all face losses and the longer we live, the more of those losses we will experience. How we face and recover from them has everything to do with the health and vibrancy of the life we live.

Please join me as I tell you about the journey Marty and I shared and what I learned along the way about human resiliency in the face of great loss.

CHAPTER 1, COUNSELOR'S RESPONSE

In this chapter: Marv writes about his childhood and the years building his career and a family. He tells us about the bullying he experienced as a child, the rejection he felt by his family and about his failed marriages. We learn about the joy he experienced when he fell in love with Marty—only to lose her to cancer. Acknowledging the previous "losses" is part of the grieving process for his wife of 19 years.

Importance: Grief is cumulative. If we have losses from our past that are still unresolved and painful, it's important to notice what those losses are. It will bring insight to our present situation to revisit them—with a trusted friend or a counselor—and specifically identify them. The helpfulness comes from seeing similarities in the feelings of sadness we hold for the past losses as they compare to the current events. These feelings feed into some seemingly simplistic but usually very powerful conclusions that create our beliefs.

Clinical insights: When we experience loss, our bodies react. Many symptoms of loss experienced throughout our lives can rest within our bodies for decades unaddressed but, as we experience consecutive similar events, we are sure to be reminded of sadness from our past. Triggers —familiar sights, sounds or feelings—can send us directly back to old, deep wounds. Your body may remind you through physical sensations.

"Common complaints include fatigue and inability to sleep well. . . . waking up at night and not being able to get back to sleep. The body also reacts to the fight by giving us signals, registering sensations that are symbols of the conflict that is ensuing." Thomas Golden, *Swallowed by a Snake.*

This is particularly true of men. Grief affects the cognitive state, and men in particular report a decline in their capacity to concentrate and a loss of short term memory. Others experience their lowest levels of self-esteem.

Grief work is counter to the western way of thinking because it requires the griever to take time to pay attention to their feelings, to 'hold on to' those emotions, and to process the loss, usually while being required to return to work within a matter of days or a short week. The question for a grieving person is 'Do you have the skills to manage the accumulation of emotions you're feeling, especially if you are aware that you're holding on to past losses, and can you regulate your response to sadness?' The importance of this is in making sure the grieving person has the ability to remain safe and healthy.

Suggestions: Those of you experiencing loss now, allow yourself to feel the discomfort of the past losses with no judgment about them or about yourself. As simple as this sounds, it really does help to know what is actually making us sad. An acceptance of "no wonder I feel so down," can help you not be pushed by the feeling but to see it clearly, understand it and make a decision as to what you want to do with it.

The decision to let yourself recognize whatever sadness and pain still exists, no matter how long ago the loss occurred, can help bring self-compassion and understanding to the surface. That has the possibility of relieving some long-held tension, making available more energy for you to face the present.

A next step is to determine which beliefs about past losses did or didn't help us face each day. Notice which beliefs brought, and might still bring, joy, hope, or energy to you. Ask yourself which beliefs are helpful to hold on to and carry forward and which have no value and need to be let go.

Chapter 2

Marty's Story

Marty was, in the most profound way, the light and love of my life. She was my wife, best friend, lover, business partner, and co-parent. In the 19 years we were together, she gave my life deep meaning and satisfaction. Marty was happy, tirelessly engaged with life, a relentless political debater on the liberal side of all issues, compassionate at her core and a nature lover.

She had a remarkable ability to focus. She was a voracious reader and could consume 500-page novels over a weekend. Sometimes I would wake up to find that Marty had stayed up all night to develop a new product or new process for our business. We mind-shared the world around us. We agreed to always let each other know our thoughts and feelings—no restrictions. Our relationship was always the number one priority for both of us. If we were good, everything was good, and all challenges could be handled.

Marty loved to be out on the water, but I could never get her interested in fishing. When we were out on the boat, she would sit up front reading a book and from time to time ask, "How's it going back there? Catching anything?" She loved the flowers she grew all around our Colorado home. I remember her stepping out on the deck to scold the deer who were eating her Columbine.

Thinking of her love for nature, I remember our first anniversary, as we sat on a cliff on the Caribbean island of Bonaire drinking champagne, watching colorful Parrot Fish swimming below us, and watching the sunset. So many sweet, sweet memories.

I reflect on her life and our life together and remember what she taught me about living in the here and now, that being happy is a decision, how to be grateful just to be alive as a human being, and how to die with courage. Although I believe I knew her better than anyone, I find it challenging to write her story in a single chapter and in a way that speaks to her resiliency in the face of devastating loss—the loss of her own life. I want to do her story justice and provide you, the reader, with the most valuable insights from her courage and love of life.

Even though she has passed away she continues to be my greatest and most generous teacher. Marty's personal story is one of a life well-lived despite early trauma and setbacks. The positive currents running through her life are central to the larger story of her ultimate resiliency.

She had the ability to accept her situation at face value, whatever that happened to be and to make well-reasoned decisions as to how she would view and respond to events. I found her ability to weigh options and make choices about how she would deal with every aspect of her life to be remarkable and unusual. But she would say, and I would agree, that we all have the capacity to decide how we respond to life's events.

The most fundamental choice Marty made over and over again during her life was to be happy. That is as profound as it is simple. When we decided to spend our lives together, she said she had one request. I asked what that was, and she told me, "To be happy, you have to decide to be happy." Until then I hadn't realized that it was such a straightforward decision. Throughout her life, and especially at difficult moments, she steadied herself with her decision to be happy and it guided her actions going forward.

You will hear more in this and later chapters about her remarkable response to the news that she had cancer from which there was no escape. Let me say briefly that she considered happiness to be less a matter of circumstance than of a way of living, a way of being in the world where impermanence underlies everything. This core belief is behind every decision she made about how she wanted to live each day right up until she died.

EARLY LESSONS

A key decision point came when she was a young woman. As a 9 year-old schoolgirl, she had been sexually abused. As is true about so many adults who have experienced this trauma when they were young, Marty had buried her memories, grief and fears about the events, until they reemerged suddenly. When she was 30 years old, remembrance of the abuse and her abuser came flooding into her consciousness. She was re-traumatized all over again. Wisely, she put herself through an intensive course of individual and group therapy. What she learned in those settings had a lasting effect on the rest of her life. She was able to change everything about the way she viewed the original experience and the trauma of remembering it all over again. Equally important, she made two decisions that have served her well all through her life.

One was to forgive her abuser (a 'family friend') and her family for not protecting her as a child. This ability to decide how she thought about those traumatic events allowed her to let go of the memories, the distress, the complex feelings that came from these events, and to move forward a whole human being.

The second was to decide she was not going to live the life of a victim. She had been surrounded in her therapy group by people who saw themselves as wounded casualties. This was at a time and in a popular culture that focused on victimhood. But to live the life of a victim, she realized, would irreparably diminish her life.

Letting go was perhaps Marty's greatest talent, and her saving grace. It let her be happy in the moment. She did not look back or second-guess herself. She released the pain, the anger and the negative emotions of those terrible events. Deciding to let go meant that the toxicity of those experiences did not stick to her. In 19 years, though we talked about them, I never heard resentment, guilt or regret about the terrible experiences she had had as a young girl. In the work she did on herself when those memories came up, she had been able to let go of the resentments or fearful parts with grace and compassion, allowing her to live her life fully.

Marty married while she was an undergraduate at the University of Texas in Austin. In her last semester, she became pregnant with her first child. When her son Chris was born, she was three credit hours shy of graduating. She was so darn happy and so fulfilled by becoming a mother, she never went back to earn those three credits. Even without the official completion of a bachelor's degree, she went on to have a vibrant and successful career in Austin City government. She simply decided that she had made the right decision and would not let the lack of a degree stand in her way. Repeatedly during her decade-long career in Austin City government, she was tapped for positions and appointments, even though the requirements included a college degree. Clearly, she was seen by those around her as the best person to perform the job.

Marty must have decided early in her life that it was wrong to judge others, and she carried that with her throughout her life. She never felt it was her place, right or purpose to judge others. I believe that evolved during her school years when she went to 17 different schools between kindergarten and her senior year in high school. Her father, whom Marty described as a wonderful Daddy, was a serial entrepreneur who kept the family moving from place to place, mostly back and forth between locations in Ohio and Arizona. I recall her story of how they moved to Toltec, Arizona to open a Culligan water softener dealership. After everyone in the small town had one, the business was over, and they moved again. As the perpetual 'new kid' in school, she saw, heard and experienced an abundance of arbitrary criticism of herself and others. She felt that was wrong. She would rather suspend judgment and give others a chance.

Suspending judgment means that you don't waste the time or the mental and emotional energy it takes to evaluate others in a negative way. For Marty, it meant that "judgment" did not sap her energy, energy that she used to be happy and to build her own resiliency.

From early in our years together, Marty and I studied Buddhism and practiced Zen meditation. In 2000, I went to Nepal to climb, trek and study. Later we both studied and practiced at a Zen Dojo in Hawaii ,where we studied impermanence, compassion, and the connectedness of all things. One of our Zen teachers used the phrase 'suspend judgment' as a way of showing compassion for others. I used to say that Marty was born out of the belly of Buddha because she was so compassionate, able to let go of negative thoughts and experiences, and suspend judgment toward almost everyone.

Mary Torrans Lathrap, the famous women's suffragette, also

addressed this issue in her 1985 poem originally titled 'Judge Softly.' Two of the several wisdom-filled stanzas read:

Just walk a mile in his moccasins
Before you abuse, criticize and accuse.
If just for one hour, you could find a way
To see through his eyes, instead of your own muse.

....

Remember to walk a mile in his moccasins
And remember the lessons of humanity taught to you
    by your elders.
We will be known forever by the tracks we leave
In other people's lives, our kindnesses and generosity.
Take the time to walk a mile in his moccasins.

Suspending judgment does not mean you stop seeing people or events as they are. Rather, it means that you hold them in your heart as they are, not as you wish or think they should be.

Suspending judgment is not as easy as saying it. Doing so, however, is an essential aspect of loving others. Suspending judgment for the people we love is relatively easy. Extending it to others is more challenging. As Mary Lathrap suggests, we should take care not to criticize, gossip about or cast aspersions on someone when we have not walked in their moccasins. Marty and I were able to suspend judgment of each other from the beginning, and that was a core of our relationship. What does that mean, and how is it a part of Marty's story?

THE HARD PART
The first stop on the long cancer journey began in the hospital in

our hometown of Gunnison, Colorado, where MRIs revealed a spread of cancer in her neck and her hips. Knowing we were heading to Penrose Hospital in Colorado Springs, the local emergency room doctor was concerned that Marty's hips could break getting in and out of our Chevy pickup and set up an ambulance to take her there. During the 3-hour ambulance ride from Gunnison to the hospital in Colorado Springs, Marty decided to let go of all daily life concerns. She confided this to her stepson, Seth, telling him during the ride she could literally see those concerns leave her body. It gave her a lightness to be completely present and dedicate her energy to fighting the cancer. She told Seth that the trickle of tears she shed during the ride were not due to sadness or fear of cancer, but rather the tears were from gratitude that her life was so beautiful.

We learned the hard truth on our first day in the hospital. Marty was diagnosed with stage 4 lung cancer. The Penrose Hospital Director of Radiation Oncology came to our room on the second day and told us that Marty had 30 lesions on her brain and that without radiation treatments she would have but a single month to live. Our wonderfully compassionate and honest oncologist, Dr. Jesal Patel, told us on that same day that the disease would kill her and that there was no cure. The deep-seated beliefs she had lived by throughout her life formed the bedrock of the resiliency that got both of us through those early days of diagnosis and prognosis. They kept us going and our hearts open through the remaining nine months of her life.

Frail and ill as she later became, she embraced, accepted and celebrated her life. She suspended any judgment about what was happening to her. She knew if she did that, she would avoid spending her energy on self-pity or regrets. She could spend her remaining days being happy. Marty's decision to let go of worries or concerns about daily life gave her tremendous freedom to love and appreciate each day she had. I learned from her that we all have the power to make decisions about how we will react or respond to what happens to us.

Without saying so, she decided she would not complain about her cancer, the pain or the impermanence of her life. In the nine months from her diagnosis to her passing away, she never uttered a single word of complaint. That decision freed her spirit to enjoy each moment, each day, unencumbered by self-pity and to live her life fully and happily every day in spite of the cancer. Whether it was to sit in her wheelchair in the morning and enjoy coffee and orange juice while watching the deer out of our front window or to laugh with her caregivers over some silly joke, she found joy in everyday events. The height of this joy was at its purest the night we stepped out on our front deck, and she looked up at the Milky Way and said, "This is the Universe that is going to give me more life."

We had long before accepted the impermanence of life. Dr. Patel, Marty's oncologist, shared with me after Marty died that cancer patients seem to be able to decide when they die and who will be with them when they pass. She faced life and death with so much courage and chose how she wanted to go. She let me know she wanted to die in my arms. She loved to feel our shared body heat. The moment she died, I held her chest to chest, bare skin to bare skin. She always liked to be held with my arms around her, as she held her forearms together in front between us. That is how I held her as she passed from this life, just as she had wanted.

She and I had long ago decided that we weren't afraid of death. It makes no sense to be afraid of something we don't really know or understand, like death, or have any knowledge about what happens after.

That is how I know Marty was not afraid of death or of dying. The only thing fearful to her was that it would happen without her knowing it was near. So, we made it a practice in the final weeks and days to talk about how close it might be. That helped her remain calm.

"Everything can be taken from a man but one thing: the last of the human freedoms—to choose one's attitude in any given set of circumstances, to choose one's own way." These are the words of the great psychiatrist and Holocaust survivor Viktor Frankl.

To decide how we will see or respond to our losses is a fundamental human trait and choice. How we respond, whether and how we tap into our resilience, will have everything to do with how or if we recover. The loss of a loved one never leaves us, the grief does not somehow evaporate, it becomes part of us as we move forward, changed but stronger.

My own resiliency, though often flawed, comes directly from how Marty lived and loved others. Because of the decisions she had made for her life, she treated others with acceptance, compassion and love. Because she didn't spend time judging others, she had time to see them as they were and loved them anyway. Because she had been a victim, she had compassion for others, knowing in some way or another they had losses, too. Because she had decided to be happy, not even cancer could take away her happiness at being alive. Because she had decided not to be afraid of death, she gave all of us around her the courage to face her death. She loved with an open heart and taught me everything I know about how to live and how to die. Thank you, Marty.

CHAPTER 2, COUNSELOR'S RESPONSE

In this chapter: When I was helping to care for Marty during her last weeks and days, what stands out to me was her personal choice to maintain a positive attitude. She decided to accept and be gracious towards everyone who cared for her. Marv writes about how important this was for both Marty and for him. He also delves into the joys of his relationship with Marty, her "happiness" promise and his appreciation of how special a person she was. As Marv was grieving, he drew pictures and journaled his feelings and was actively creating his own process of trying to make sense of something seemingly senseless. He was actively engaged in remembering, and he was also honoring Marty.

Importance: Whether we are healthy or ill, we have the capacity to be a role model. We have the choice—and this is true for both the dying and for the loved ones left behind—of accessing our inner discourse or guiding principles, of choosing how to react to thoughts, emotions or set of circumstances. We can find it within ourselves to offer a response of gratitude to those around us. This is challenging when we are facing the enormity of a loss of a loved one and how we face a future without our beloved.

The stories Marv recorded about his relationship with Marty are part of his therapeutic process. His writing preserves precious memories that otherwise may be lost. Writing this story allowed Marv to begin assimilating, absorbing his pain along with the joy of his memories. It's his gift to Marty, to himself, and to us.

Clinical information: Loss has been defined as losing "your sense of safety and security, the meaning of your life, your physical health, your ability to relate with others, your identity, your self-esteem, or someone or something you love. Loss leads to grief." (*The PTSD Workbook*, Mary Beth Williams and Soili Poijula). The type of loss we are talking about here is the loss of a person. It is painful, terrible and irreparable. The natural response to loss is grief. Grief is a very uniquely individual experience for each of us. For many, it is a dark, narrow and winding passage through which we must travel to continue the task of living. One hard reality of loss with its ensuing feelings of grief is that the more attached we are and the more deeply we love, the more intense will be our sadness and sense of loss.

As noted in the previous chapter, another reality of loss and grief is that we seem to carry forward all of the experiences we've had of past losses. There is a pattern we've developed to deal or not to deal with them. From seemingly small daily setbacks to significant, life-changing losses, every event we experience contributes to the establishment of this pattern of response within us. This is how we learn to handle grief. We establish a pattern, healthy or not, of facing it or burying it. Deep beneath this pattern of response lies the beliefs we hold about life and loss.

"Between stimulus and response there is a space. In that space is our power to choose our response. In our response lies our growth and our freedom." —Viktor E. Frankl, Austrian <u>neurologist</u>, <u>psychiatrist</u>, <u>philosopher</u> and <u>Holocaust survivor</u>.

Suggestions: You can create a tangible memorial to your loved one by writing, drawing, creating music or dance—in short, by choosing any creative interest or skill you might have. Ultimately, you are creating a commemorative that can be shared. This activity may help ground you, as it requires thought and focus—you're thinking and remembering who and what you have lost. Because you are involved in a focused activity, your heart and mind can slowly, and, hopefully, gently, assimilate the difficulty of the pain that is felt alongside treasured memories.

Our culture is a little short on established, meaningful rituals, but your response may be as simple as taking a walk to a favorite location where you can offer your thoughts or sing a song to your loved one. It could be the lighting of a candle in the privacy of your home and reading a favorite poem that you enjoy. A ritual can be any creative action that adds meaning to a time of remembering. Whether you choose to present something you've made to them, figuratively speaking, or you offer a thoughtful presentation, it is an offering. It gives you a way to say, "You'll never be forgotten." Memorializing helps us hold on to the memories. We can hold our loved one's presence within us, forever if we want, in all of its goodness and with all of its difficulties.

CHAPTER 3

THE END AND THE BEGINNING

Thank you for joining us on this journey. I want to share more about our cancer journey, because Marty's courage and open-hearted approach to life is best understood in the harsh light of what she actually experienced.

In the summer of 2016, Marty needed help for the pain she was experiencing in her neck. Over the previous several months, we had gone to a local doctor several times, each time for new pains in her hips, neck, back, shoulders or elbows.

As the pain intensified, she started seeing Dr. Scott Ross, a pain management doctor in Colorado Springs, which was a 3 ½ hour drive from our home in Gunnison. At first, the procedure he used brought some relief, but then the pain came back a few weeks later. We drove back to Colorado Springs to see Dr. Ross a second time. He became very concerned and ordered an MRI of Marty's brain. When I asked Dr. Ross what he was uneasy about, I heard the word "cancer" for the first time.

We had the MRI of her brain that same day in Colorado Springs and then drove the 3 ½ hours back home to Gunnison.

We had to return the next day for a neck MRI that Dr. Ross had ordered. As we were driving to the Gunnison hospital that next morning, Dr. Ross called to tell us that the MRI of her brain showed that Marty had multiple cancerous lesions and tumors on her brain. I was at the wheel of the car when I took the call. Have you heard the phrase "my stomach dropped"? That is what I felt. I felt my heart stop beating and my stomach drop out the bottom of my body. I parked the truck, put Dr. Ross on speaker so he could tell us both. We held each other and cried.

We named it what it was, cancer, in the first few minutes to immerse ourselves in the reality of our situation. We would face it head on and together.

In a phone call, in a single moment, we dealt with the devastating news that all cancer patients experience. The future literally went away and the past no longer mattered. After two more MRI's and two more phone calls that same day, we now knew that the cancer, which was later diagnosed as lung cancer, had metastasized in Marty's brain, neck and hips. The pains she had wouldn't go away.

Dr. Ross let us know what we needed to know. His discovery meant that we would have several more months to be together in this life. To this day, he is our hero. I still see him for shots for pain in my lower back and each time I go to see him, I take him a bottle of his favorite champagne.

It has been hard to look back and think about the local doctors who guessed it was arthritis, or who gave her a shot in the hip to see if that worked. The lack of referrals to specialists over those six months before we saw Dr. Ross contributed to the advance of her cancer and to our emotional pain, including some initial anger, after learning it was cancer.

When Dr. Ross and I talked after the second and third MRIs,

he suggested we come to Penrose for treatment. He was director of pain management at the hospital and assured us we would be well taken care of. As we prepared to make the long trip from our home to Penrose, the emergency room doctor at the local hospital said that Marty needed to be transported to Penrose by ambulance because her hips could "easily break" getting in and out of our pickup. We both thought out loud about all the times she had gotten in and out of the truck!

From the moment we arrived at Penrose Hospital, Marty was so pleased to still be alive and was ready to do everything she could to extend the life she loved. The experience she had in the ambulance would free her to be present and happy, in spite of the diagnosis, the pain and the predictable outcome, during the rest of her life.

I don't remember all of the drive while I followed the ambulance with Marty in it—it was the hardest one of my life—but I do remember talking with our stalwart friends Raechel, Andy and Tam, and, of course, my son Seth. These friends, family and others would be the people who would see us through what was to come. Of course, I also spoke with Marty's children, Chris and Emily, as soon as we got to the hospital and kept them up to date and engaged throughout all of it.

It was a terrifying time. The morning after we arrived, a Saturday, the doctor who was the head of radiation oncology came to our room and told us that unless Marty received whole-brain radiation, she would be dead in a month. That same afternoon, our oncologist, Dr. Patel, came to our room and with great compassion and honesty told us that there was no known cure for Marty's type of cancer. The next day, Marty had her first of two surgeries to place titanium pins in her hip to prevent it from breaking. The pace of news, treatments and adjustments was stunning and overwhelming.

I remember feeling out of my body that first morning at Penrose Hospital. When I walked outside the hospital to move our truck from the Emergency Room parking space, I remember looking down and seeing my feet moving: I was walking, but I couldn't feel my feet or my body. I was literally outside my body. This was real. It was trauma and my mind was trying to defend against what it couldn't take in, what I could not handle. The episode of feeling outside myself finally ended. I didn't leave my body again.

Dr. Ross had been right about the care we would receive at Penrose. The compassion of the doctors and nurses on the oncology floor, in radiation, in surgery, was truly amazing. One of many memories is when a brilliant young oncology nurse sat on Marty's bedside in the middle of the night holding both of Marty's hands in hers, looking into her eyes as she cried, and listened for two hours as Marty expressed her fears.

I had a cot in the hospital room, but I don't think I actually slept for the first three days. That was the beginning of becoming hyper-vigilant, listening for any change in Marty's breathing that signaled a change in her pain level or that she was crying in her sleep.

Marty's love of her life, and determination to live as long and as well as she could, set a course of aggressive testing and treatment.

The nine months following the diagnosis was a time full of every possible emotion. As close and intimate as our relationship had been for the previous 19 years, being a cancer patient and being the one taking care of her all day and night is the most intimate two people can be with each other. We fell more deeply in love with each other every day.

The intimacy of finishing Marty's sentences when she

couldn't, of fixing meals and sitting in front of the windows eating breakfast, of giving comfort and care, of sharing ALL of our emotions and holding nothing back, of knowing we only have today made impermanence become palpable.

Cancer is not one diagnosis. It is many. With every test to determine the status of the cancer, we got another diagnosis. Another prognosis. The day we learned that Marty did not have the genetic markers to make the new immunotherapy an option was nearly as difficult as the day we learned she had cancer. I was devastated, my chest lurched, and I wept openly with just the three of us in Dr. Patel's office. Each test, each operation, each next piece of news, is another 'diagnosis moment.' Some cancer patients, thankfully, hear some good news along the way, and some even hear, "you are cancer free."

Cancer is a journey. Each moment presents an opportunity to face our emotions head-on and embrace them, whatever they are. Those moments became part of the grieving process for Marty and me. In our case, because the diagnosis always moved in the wrong direction, each of those moments presented a loss for us to deal with. We grieved, and later accepted each one as they occurred.

Marty was a very independent person and a mature woman who owned her own life. She had to let me take care of her. As the cancer progressed, I lifted her into bed and into her wheelchair, took her to the toilet, to her piano bench, to the couch. When we sat in our oncologist's office and heard the news that she was not a candidate for immunotherapy, I cried when she couldn't. As time passed from the whole-brain radiation, I finished her sentences when she couldn't. I fixed food she liked when she could not. I did the laundry and appreciated that she had done that all those years.

She let me bathe her and tidy her after bathroom duties. We picked out fun stocking caps during the winter months. She let me lift her into the truck seat beside me for our journeys into town. She didn't mind when I resurrected my race car driver skills to get her the hospital fast when she was in trouble. She let herself be taken care of. She let me take care of her.

Cancer patients and many people who are experiencing debilitating conditions or illnesses are put in a position of allowing others to take care of them. Because Marty was so independent and at the same time loving, I was poignantly aware of what it took for her to allow this. She gave herself over to me, to trust me, to love me by letting me take care of her. She gave me that gift.

I gave her the gift of taking care of her in all the ways and more that I have mentioned here. I didn't do it alone. We were fortunate to be referred by local home health services to Bre, a wonderful, professional caregiver. She was there with us on and off during the last several months and stayed with us all the time for the last several weeks of Marty's life. Bre made it possible for me to be a husband and not a caregiver all of the time. Most hospice or other home health organizations can orchestrate this type of in-home care. Bre also gave me occasional respite for a few hours or a day of fishing or hunting.

Bre and Marty loved each other. Bre would come into the bedroom and say, "Hi, beautiful!" and Marty would say, "Hi gorgeous!" They laughed and joked when she took her meds or drank tea with Bre. Bre was born in Ireland and brought with her the humor and ferocity of an Irish lass. She would say that Irish women never lose their temper—they always know where to find it!

She was a perfect fit for us. I refer to her and others who do what she does as 'end of life workers.' They are a special group of people who can be compassionate, completely involved and somehow survive the experience over and over. She and I have remained good friends, bonded by our shared experiences with Marty.

Likewise, home health nurses had a profound impact on our ability to provide the level of care Marty needed. They were like angels walking in the door to set up an IV or give us support and instructions for Marty's care. As events progressed, they transitioned to provide hospice care for Marty's last weeks and days. Their compassion and caregiving were both physically and emotionally healing. I will never forget them. They answered our questions and, as Marty's time grew near, they guided me through the difficult decisions I faced, such as when to stop giving IV fluids.

Marty had been clear about her wishes and one of the nurses in particular, Aline, brought me comfort as I had to weigh what to do and when. I knew I loved Marty enough to carry out her wishes to their natural conclusion, but I surely needed guidance about when and how. And I needed morale support as those times unfolded. Aline, Bre, and others provided that, and I am so grateful for their calm and compassionate guidance.

There are probably people and resources you can connect with in your community, whether you are a patient or the caregiver. This is essential to surviving the experience of a debilitating disease. Of course, family members often provide this care. Be aware that family members providing this level of care also need to function in their other role as a husband, wife or child.

I found that I was helped by having that time to be Marty's husband. My memories of caregiving are many, but the times when we could just be together, while Bre or others provided the personal care Marty needed, are those that I cherish the most.

Caregivers and the cancer patients they are caring for experience a sort of intimacy that is unique. Having someone carry you from the bed to the wheelchair and onto the toilet or couch, requires trust, letting go of your own body and your ability to move yourself physically in space. And in every touch, look and movement, the caretaker can express deep respect, tenderness and gentle care for the person who is experiencing these losses. At the same time, a caregivers pain, exhaustion and need for support is real.

For lovers, like Marty and me, the intimacy that grows during this caregiving and receiving time is not like anything else. We had a wonderful nineteen-year love affair, romance and had experienced the wonder of long-term love in the context of marriage. Our intimacy, we would say, was complete—intellectual, emotional, spiritual and physical. In every touch, look and movement, we expressed deep respect, tenderness, love and gentle care for each other. The emotional and physical intimacy we experienced during Marty's cancer illness was deeper and more spiritual than anything we had ever experienced.

We developed the ability to communicate paragraphs by looking into each other's eyes. A touch, a hand squeeze, a pat, an arm around the shoulders, spoke volumes of love poems. We would laugh so hard sometimes when I lifted her into bed, grunted or landed on the bed with her. When I would hand her a glass of orange juice as we looked out the window into the morning light, her doe eyes said thank you and I love you without a word passing our lips.

The intimacy we experienced during this time became our bond for eternity, a constancy of existence that made it possible for us to stay connected beyond suffering and beyond death.

Marty died from the lung cancer. I held her in my arms as she took her last breath. She literally freed herself from the cancer on Independence Day, July 4, 2017.

We held a service 10 days or so later when family and friends gathered to celebrate her beautiful life, to thank her for her love, her kindness and for teaching us all so much about how to live and how to die with courage.

The day Marty passed is the beginning of my journey of loss, grief and finding the resiliency to reconstruct my life.

CHAPTER 3, COUNSELOR'S RESPONSE

In this chapter: When Marv and Marty heard the terrifying diagnosis of Marty's cancer, they made a decision to join forces to fight this disease. It was crucial that they discover how to move beyond the impasse that can be created by our initial human response, which is to push away the truth. Marv said, "We decided to call it what it was," and they expressed out loud, "It's cancer." With a strong agreement to always speak honestly about their feelings and not to wallow in anger over missed diagnoses, they could move forward on a search for what to do next.

Importance: Receiving the frightening news that you or your loved one has a disease can flood you with a mixture of feelings.

Shock: Your body may freeze up or become numb or you may feel you've left your body (a phenomenon referred to as dissociation, specifically depersonalization). Shock prevents us from absorbing most of the information that we hear. We need time to process bad news like this.

Disbelief: It seems impossible that life can be calm and routine one moment and then be disrupted beyond imagination.

Recent theory describes the movement of our thoughts, as they shift back and forth between a focus on the reality of our loss with its pain and a focus on the need for restoration as "oscillation;" a healthy activity that works to restore a sense of emotional balance (Stroebe and Shut, Dual Process Model, 1999).

Psychological distancing: This occurs within us. From it comes a natural cushioning within our brain that gives us space and time to take in only as much information as is manageable. Distancing cannot be maintained for very long because an awareness of 'time' is also part of this experience.

Anger. Anger can sideline us or be a way to serve our needs. An unhealthy use of anger might be a vengeful, retaliatory response that consumes a lot of energy. A healthy anger can motivate you towards gaining clarity and accuracy about the illness or the event. We can make a deliberate choice between the two.

Marv and Marty used anger in a healthy way. They had to decide what to do with their anger over receiving an incorrect diagnosis and having "wasted time." They were able to set aside the destructive, retaliatory use of anger and chose the more constructive, fact-seeking use. That choice gave them freedom both to conserve needed energy and to focus on gaining assistance from credible resources.

Clinical information: Sadness over a potential loss or loss itself can develop into depression. Medically, *depression* is identified as an illness, not an emotion, but many of its so-called symptoms are feelings we experience with grief. There is a difference between feeling depressed due to grief and developing what is referred to as Major Depressive Disorder (MDD). The Diagnostic and Statistical Manual of Mental Disorders (DSM-5) notes that it is important to differentiate between MDD (the

Disorder), MDE (the Episode), and Grief, because their treatment is different.

"In distinguishing Grief from a Major Depressive Episode (MDE), it is useful to consider that in Grief the predominant effect is feelings of emptiness and loss, while in MDE it is persistent depressed mood and the inability to anticipate happiness or pleasure." (DSM-5, page 161, footnote 1).

Neither depression nor the sadness that comes from grief is something to handle alone. A support group or counselor can help you regain some sense of control and feel better.

As to the out-of-body experience (depersonalization) that Marv described, it is defined as "the experience of feeling detached from, and as if one is an outside observer of, one's mental processes, body, or actions (e.g., feeling like one is in a dream; a sense of unreality of self, perceptual alterations, emotional and/ or physical numbing; temporal distortions; sense of unreality)." Diagnostic and Statistical Manual of Mental Disorders (DSM-5).

Suggestions: If you find yourself where Marv and Marty found themselves—facing progressing illness and confusion as to how long a future lay ahead—then you've already felt a whirlwind of painful emotions and a nearly debilitating fear. I recommend Teri Collet's booklet for hospice families, "Making the Most of Every Moment, A Patient's Guide to Living with Hospice."

You may also find that within the mixed-up response to getting bad news comes the "How did this happen?" and "Why is it happening to me or to him or to her?" questions. Feeling that "It's not right!" or "This isn't fair!" is common. Many people have shared with me that they feel they caused the illness somehow or that they're being punished for something they did or didn't do. These are normal questions and perceptions. You need to know you did not cause the illness—it isn't your fault. You are not being punished. The chaos of unanswerable questions can easily give way to overpowering and extended sadness.

I recommend you take a look at the many helpful suggestions in "Coping with the Loss of a Loved One", a pamphlet put out by the American Cancer Society.

CHAPTER 4

BEING ALIVE
TAKES COURAGE

After a profound loss it takes courage to keep going, to continue living. In the weeks following Marty's passing, I was faced with the decision whether or not to go forward with life. One of those poignant moments came on the day I finished designing our gravestone. More about the design itself later.

As I sat at the computer in the design room at the memorial shop, I could feel the tears coming, the sadness rising in my chest, my breathing being affected. Tears flowed right along with the design ideas for the gravestone, and as the master engraver made it all come to life on his computer screen, I felt joyful and sad at the same time. Joyful that the gravestone would express what was important for Marty's memory and that it would be there for our children to see when they came to pay their respects. Sadly, the stone was a beautiful but stark reminder that Marty was gone.

When the design was exactly as I wanted it—and after expressing my gratitude to the designer for his help—I headed west out of town to sit by the river. The skies that day were the deep blue that only Colorado can produce, and the Gunnison

River was streaming by in its never-ending flow to become part of the Colorado River. I knew what was coming, and I wanted to be out in nature to face it.

Sitting there on a bench warmed by the sun on a beautiful August day, the understanding that Marty was gone deepened. It wasn't that I had been in denial of her passing. The new reality was seeping down into my body, brain and heart, like water seeking its own level.

I cried for two hours, tears running, chest heaving at times, sobbing in the afternoon sun. A couple walking by asked if I was okay. The physical and emotional pain was wrenching. It came as a surprise to me that I still had a ways to go to fully accept the loss.

As the reality seeped into my soul that afternoon, I was faced with the decision to go on without her—or not. I faced this question more than once. Each time I made the same decision—to go on living.

The way it happened that August afternoon was that I noticed several flocks of geese flying overhead and looked up to watch them. I realized in that moment that life, like the geese, was going to go on with me or without me and that I wanted to go with it—full and flat out. I would have to be myself.

The alternative, as I saw it in those moments, was to accept the loss but shrink my life, sink into depression and hopelessness and have no real purpose in being here. That choice meant giving up in the face of the most profound pain I had ever experienced.

The choice to let go into the pain felt like the easier, more inviting choice—to let it take me and not fight against the sadness. But the resiliency that had always been within me showed itself in that moment. Like the geese flying overhead, I would go on.

I made two decisions in the sun that afternoon. One, I would move forward with life, whatever that might bring. Second, I would live life fully with an open heart.

While working on the gravestone brought up the reality of Marty's passing, in retrospect, it gave me an opportunity to face and accept her passing in a very deep way. I felt very alone that day, but at least I had made two critical, forward-leaning decisions. As significant as the decisions were, it was equally essential to rediscover the powerful life force within me that I now call resiliency.

THE DECISION TO BE HAPPY

Sitting by the river that day, I knew deep down that at some point I would be faced with additional decisions on how I wanted to 'be' in what remained of this life—happy or something less.

Later in December of that year, I took a solo trip to Australia and New Zealand. I referred to that trip as 'my resiliency tour.' The idea was to travel to a place I'd never been and where I knew no one, to put myself out there and get comfortable in the world again. Traveling alone was a way, and continues to be a way, for me to build resiliency in myself. A part of the reason solo travel helped me so much is that traveling alone meant that I had to interact with the people I met along the way, rather than primarily with a person I was traveling with. Travel gives me courage to be a human being in the world, wherever I may be on the planet.

On the backside of the trip to Australia and New Zealand, I spent two weeks driving the coastline of New Zealand's South Island. A week or so into that part of the trip, I landed in Te Anau in the southwest part of the island. Walking the shore of Lake Te Anau, watching a beautiful New Zealand sunrise take shape on New Year's Day, 2018, I decided to be happy.

I missed Marty terribly on that trip, and each one since. But traveling alone continues to help get me back to my gregarious self, reengaging with people and the world around me. I have continued to travel solo.

For me, and maybe for you too, the decision to live is one thing and how to live is another. My decision to go on with life was made in the midst of profound physical and emotional grief from losing Marty to cancer. The timing of the decision to go on is what made it so important to me. It could have gone either way at that point, and, because my resiliency showed up at that vulnerable time, the decision gave me a lot of courage to go forward.

Each day since I sat there beside the river, I have been consciously aware of my motivation, desire if you will, to move toward and choose happiness. Some days are more successful than others, but it is my overall direction, and I know it is what Marty would want. Walking the shores of Lake Te Anau was another time I made the resolution to be happy. Marty had asked that I make a decision to be happy before we got engaged. Clever girl.

WAVES

Accepting a loss is a process with no particular end. For me, and many others, the analogy of ocean waves works when I try to describe grief. At first and for several weeks after Marty passed, it felt like the waves were 100 feet tall and came one after another, crashing me against the rocks of sadness. After a time, the waves came less frequently, then the waves continued but not quite as big and powerful, maybe 80 feet, but still coming and creating a crash on the rocks. Over time, the waves would become less frequent and less crushing. When I was in New Zealand, six months after Marty passed, the waves came less frequently and with less velocity. Now, five years later, they still come once in a while, with less crushing weight.

Physical, emotional and intellectual acceptance also comes in wave-like moments. Sometimes the waves of acceptance are big, burly waves, like the tearful one at the river watching the geese fly over. Other times, the waves of acceptance are more nuanced, but nonetheless powerful and emotional. As I got more used to waking up and going to sleep alone or being able to face going to the grocery store, or fixing and eating dinner alone, those were experiences of acceptance and were emotional, especially the first several times.

WAVES NOT STAGES

For me, there were no stages of grief, as most of us had earlier understood grief. I found it to be an organic process and experience. For instance, I never suffered emotions other than sadness. I didn't feel anger, denial, guilt or shame. And there has been no real order to what I experienced. I did try to bargain while Marty was alive: I asked the universe to give the cancer to me. I would take it. Of course, that didn't happen.

Contrary to traditional common wisdom, grief has no timeline. Everyone's grief is different and unique. My own experience is that the grief changed and continues to change over time, and that the loss never really goes away. I have learned how to incorporate it as a part of me and to manage it as part of my life.

My love of Marty continues and always will. The same is true of the loss. It is on me to keep moving forward, reconstructing life with all the resiliency I can muster.

The emotions of grief come up, still, organically and I let them be expressed at the moment they come up. Acceptance sometimes came from within me, from a preconscious place, for the most part. That was inborn resiliency expressing itself. I observe it happening in real time, like walking or driving alone and realizing I was okay. It feels like my mind, heart and body accepted the truth at a pace that I could tolerate.

But I have also been very consciously involved in making intentional decisions to accept Marty's death. For example, when I go the cemetery and 'talk' with her I am accepting her passing.

Resiliency is the resource we have in order to live with uncertainty and not be defeated by it. Though it may not seem like it at the time, the follow-on of a loss is an extraordinary opportunity to grow and become a more complete human being, one who is more compassionate and conscious. Accepting the impermanence of all things is essential to building resiliency, an issue I will address later.

Accepting a loss is hard work. What does it mean to accept? For me it means realizing—sometimes in increments—emotionally, intellectually and physically that the loss is real. In other words, acceptance is the end of denial.

As much as it takes courage to live, it takes courage to die. Marty taught all who knew her how to live with an open heart and how to die with courage. This is her legacy.

WHEN THE ROCKS SING

In December of the year Marty passed, on the beach at Greymouth on the west coast of the South Island, NZ, I found some peace within myself. Walking the beach there for three days with the waves rhythmically rolling in, one after another, put me in a Zen meditative state. By the afternoon of the second day, my mind and heart had become quieter and calmer than any time since before Marty's diagnosis. It took a quiet mind to begin hearing the rocks sing. The waves came in one after another and on their way out, the water washing over the flat, disk-shaped rocks made them chatter against each other, making them "sing."

When I was able to be quiet enough within myself to hear the rocks sing, I knew a shift had happened. I was able to listen past the pain of the loss of Marty and be fully present in the moment. That evening, I wrote this poem in my journal and have titled the book "When the Rocks Sing."

My hope for you is that when you come to that moment in the healing process, you too will hear the rocks sing. The book title comes from this experience and this poem:

Calm and Content

How illusive
You are
My friends
Even to define you
Let alone
To be you

Would I know
You if I met you?
Not much friends
We've been these years
Except in love
Have I known you

I met you on
A rocky beach
Greymouth by name
I walked Down Under
That bird and I
Tracks in the sand for days

Driftwood thoughts
Sunset orange and
Visitors from afar
You found me there
Among the singing rocks
And waves

Life can
Be all right
Content in my skin
Calm in my heart
Present
Looking forward

Getting to know you
Still
My heart
Still
In love
With life

CHAPTER 4, COUNSELOR'S RESPONSE

In this chapter: In working his way through his profound grief, Marv asked himself whether life was worth living. That is, should he partake of life to its fullest or allow the sadness and pain of the loss to overwhelm and define him. Marv found his answer—his resiliency—in nature and in shared beliefs that he had with his wife, Marty, which the two of them had talked about over the years of their relationship. Marv made his choice to be happy, as he had once promised Marty, and to meet life head-on and with strength.

Importance: You may believe life is always worth living, no matter what, or that life holds value only under certain circumstances. You may derive strength from a faith that gives you hope for a heavenly reunion with your loved ones. You may have a strong cultural heritage that dictates what your response to death should be and what options your future holds if a loved one dies. Whatever the beliefs are, our internal self rests on them, and they either help us or hinder us as we grieve.

A profound loss runs counter to our expectations of how we think life should play out. Somewhere in our cognitive world we know loss could occur, but we don't actively anticipate that, in fact, it will. The actual experience of loss is usually beyond our control. It rips away something that had been a living, breathing part of our life, a big portion of our happiness and our future. We're forced to acknowledge, and someday perhaps, reevaluate and reestablish the beliefs we've long held as we ask ourselves how we'll survive the sadness, what will life look like now, and how we will ever manage to function.

Clinical insights: The overwhelming hurt and disorientation that comes from losing a loved one is an unpredictable experience. There can be regression that may look like preoccupation with remembrances of the loved one, feelings of numbness, confusion around almost everything, forgetfulness (as in "What's my name?" as you sign a document). There may be bouts of anxiety, nausea, headaches and general fatigue, as well as an inability to focus. Some experience uncontrolled crying, changes in appetite as well as other behaviors that are unusual for them.

These behaviors resemble depression. They comprise grief. One can feel as if they've been left out in a terrible storm. The storm does provide us with valuable information. The key to navigating this chaotic, emotional storm is to slow down, notice what you need in the moment, and then take the time to fully tend to that need. Healing for deep grief and sadness lies within the time we take to tend to it.

Suggestions: When we actively engage in regular activity (almost any kind) our body has a chance to adjust to our pain. We begin to assimilate it as we think, move, add something to our day and acknowledge that our pain can coexist beside our normal activities. Loss and pain become a legitimate, recognized, valuable part of us, some of the building blocks that add to the form of who we are. Our body, mind, and heart remember, and it's important to remember.

We as humans are generally known not to do well if left entirely alone to grieve a loss. A grief therapist can help you process through your feelings, offer support that will bring some relief simply by hearing you and suggest actions that can be taken to help you in the struggle to survive.

That said, the first decision you face is whether to allow yourself to plummet into a state of dying with your loved one or to continue living by doing whatever work is needed to find hope, purpose and meaning to guide you in the coming days. As you engage in the therapeutic process, whether with a therapist or a grief support group (often available locally as well as on the internet) and as you become active, you are considered to be "grieving" which generations past referred to as "mourning."

Grieving does have its own path and we can follow it where it leads. As the children's song, "We're Going on a Bear Hunt," says about obstacles: "We can't go over it, we can't go under it, it looks like we just have to go through it!"

You are not alone in this experience, though it may feel as if you are. You will come to see your way through this, though it seems impossible now.

CHAPTER 5

LOSS IS INEVITABLE

A compassionate death—the term could suggest the "right to die" or "assisted suicide" or other self-directed ways to pass on. While those are worthy topics, I would like to share a conversation Marty and I had two years prior to the cancer diagnosis. It was a conversation between lovers, between two people living in a happy present and brimming with good health and hope.

Marty and I were out on the front deck on a warm summer evening, enjoying the view and taking stock of the day. The pair of doves that hung around the house were cooing in the Aspen tree near the deck and, as the evening wore on, coyotes were calling from the mountain behind us. Our conversation wandered from business issues, our kids and the weather forecast to us. Holding hands as we did in companionable moments like this, Marty brought up the question of what would happen—what should we do—if one of us passed before the other.

I stopped listening to the sounds of nature around us and heard only our voices. We agreed that the one of us who remained here should move on with their life and, most importantly, be happy. In that conversation, we released each other to enjoy the rest of our life.

As usual, Marty started from a more centered place than I. Her view in that moment was larger than mine. Mine was centered at first on the certainty that I would be the first to go. I was saddened by the thought of dying and leaving her behind. It was difficult to imagine her with someone else if that became part of her happiness. I got past those feelings quickly, though, because I wanted so much for her to be happy with me or without me, which was and is my definition of love.

Our conversation and the quiet and calm understanding it brought between us, was a timeless gift. She left this world knowing that I would go on with my life and reconfirm the decision I had made years before—to be happy. While I was free to experience the full weight of the sadness of losing her, I could still move forward with what remains of this life. This is what I think of as a compassionate death.

I know Marty wants me to be happy. This is perhaps the greatest gift that we ever gave each other. It is a material manifestation of our love that has transcended death.

I think of this every day, and it informs every significant decision I make about how to live each day. I know that if it was me that was gone and she was still here, I would want the same for her. It is an essential part of our bond that lives on. That conversation was and is an affirmation that I can continue to love Marty and love others who are still here and alive. Because of this conversation, I could again find happiness, without feeling that I am betraying Marty. She and I always had agreed that the only limits on a human heart's ability to love are the ones we place on it.

This is a conversation all couples in a long-term relationship—all manner of family units—can have. Our culture doesn't necessarily encourage this kind of thinking, because it anticipates death. We know death is real, certain and an integral part of this life and yet we avoid talking about it. Facing it and dealing with it honestly, in my experience, adds a sense of urgency to live life fully.

Loss is inevitable. Having a conversation with a loved one and talking about the emotional, mental and spiritual life you wish for each other will have great significance in both of your futures. We never know who will go first. All we can do is plan and express the love that releases each other to pursue happiness and a full life after we pass. On various levels, these conversations are relevant to all the loved ones in our lives—our partners, parents, siblings, friends.

TALKING WITH MY MOM

In the last few months of my Mother's 95-year-long life—after the broken hip, going to the nursing home, losing the ability to pay her own bills—she said that she no longer felt she had a purpose. I assured her that her family was glad she was here and, while she appreciated that, she still felt that she was ready to go. I asked her how she felt about her life and her answer was classic Mom. "I would say it has been an average life." I asked her how she felt about having an average life and she said, "I'm okay with it." We laughed and we cried a little. She was gone about two weeks later.

The way she was able to look back on her life and be okay with it meant that she was content in her later years, even though there were hard things along way—the loss of her husband, of being able to live in her house, of the ability to drive her car, of outliving nearly all of her friends, of being able to live independently on so many levels.

Mom was full of piss and vinegar to the end, and would tell you straight up what she thought. She weighed 74 pounds and had shrunk from 5 feet tall to a tiny 4 feet 7 inches and wondered why people thought she was small! She didn't think of herself that way, so, for her, she wasn't small at all.

She was like a tiny, lovable Dr. Seuss character, straight out of the Depression years. Her house got electricity when she was 18, and it wasn't until she was 21 when a phone came along. When she passed, she had many hundreds of thousands of dollars sitting in a savings account, because it was safe there. It might as well have been in a coffee can buried in the backyard. She and her generational peers saved their money, because they felt secure having some. They had lived through a time when no one they knew had any money.

My folks were children of the Great Depression. Their families lost everything in the Depression. But they learned resiliency. Resiliency came in terms of working hard, saving everything and living modestly, even though for the decades following World War II, they lived in the world's historically greatest economy. Following the Depression and the staggering loss of life in the Second World War, they and their generation used the GI Bill, low interest and tax rates, and a victory in the war, to build the world's most powerful nation that we live in and enjoy today. As a generation, the Depression kids were remarkably resilient.

BORROWED TIME

The very idea of "permanence" exists in one place only: the human mind. It is backed by nothing but our wish for it to be so. I believe this is born of our love of life, of people and the natural world, and our desire for life to continue. I've always thought if I were to fall off of a tall building, that I would keep my eyes open to experience every last millisecond of my existence. My experience is that life seeks itself and wants as much of it as is possible.

The Grand Canyon has been in a steady state of change, revealing more of what lies beneath and certainly more beauty, for at least 6 million years. All I have to do is look in the mirror and know that everything is changing. Ha! Perhaps decay can be beautiful!

What lives dies, and what seems permanent is simply changing at a pace too slow for us to recognize. Life, and all that we know, exists within the timeless certainty of impermanence. The idea is that everything, literally everything, is in the constant flow of change.

Ikkyû Sojun, 1394-1481, wrote of impermanence:

The moon is a house

in which the mind is master.

Look very closely:

only impermanence lasts.

The floating world, too, will pass.

The impermanence of life itself can be unsettling. With all my heart, I did not want Marty to die. Even though she was not afraid, I was sad beyond description when it was all happening. We want life and love to continue. It is born in us and in all of life. When the American Dipper hatches her young, the bird will dive in the swiftest of waters to find and retrieve river insects so her babies can thrive. We all know better than to cross a momma bear with cubs. Life seeks to survive. As the late Michael Crichton wrote in *Jurassic Park*, "Life will find a way."

The human heart and mind can experience more than one emotion at the same time. While we can understandably be disturbed or even frightened by the impermanence of life, we can use that to experience life more fully. When we knew that Marty would die from the cancer, that created a poignant urgency to live as fully as possible every moment of the life we had left together. This was not a new concept for us, but the heightened awareness of the limited amount of our time together brought us close and more emotionally intimate than ever before. We agreed that was the most intensely intimate time of our 19 years together.

Perhaps if we look at life more as a time-limited offer, which it is, we can appreciate and live each day more intentionally. One of our doctors in Austin, Bill Jones, often said "none of us make it out of here alive." And then he proceeded to do everything he could to keep us in good health for as long as possible.

Planning for the Inevitable

Well-organized communities do emergency planning around what to do if a flood, wildfire, tsunami, earthquake, avalanche or other major disaster should happen. We prepare ourselves, so that when or if something major happens, we can recover. The speed with which a community can put itself back together—send kids back to school, return people to their homes, get business and government back up and running—is a measure of the depth of a community's resiliency. Resiliency requires planning, backups and redundancy in major systems like power and water—and practice. It takes practice to be resilient.

A notable example of the power of preparation for emergencies, even disasters, was when United Flight 232 crash-landed at the Sioux City airport in northwest Iowa on July 19, 1989. A good friend of mine, Bob Peters, was Iowa's Department of Human Services senior field director in the area. He was involved in leading the state's emergency preparedness planning and exercise. When the crash occurred, he was directly involved in the response. He said afterward that it was the training and skill of the pilot to deal with a crippled aircraft and the well-practiced response by the people on the ground that saved many lives that day.

ACCEPTANCE

The more we love, the more we have to lose. Love and loss are our constant companions. Together, they make up much of human life. Generally, though, we like one much more than other. Along the way, five months after Marty passed I wrote this:

Life, Love, Loss
All busted up
Heartbroken, crushed
Scarred deep from the Fire
Love and loss

Once I saw,
Hoped, they were separated
At birth like some
Ill-begotten twins

So much life energy
Spent
So much head fake time
Spent on the Myth
Hoping they're different

Turns out
Love and
Loss are
Fully part of the whole of it
Can't do one without the other

One and the same
Circle
Yin and Yang
In perfect proportion
Teeter totter

One can't breathe
Without
The other
Constant companions
Never separate

Love
Loss
Fire of Life

The more we can accept loss as part of life, the better we can plan for it, deal with it when it happens and recover with resiliency. Alternatively, we can live in denial, if we wish. That will ensure that we are surprised every time loss happens. Yikes! I think surprises are better left for birthdays. I think you probably share the perspective that you would rather not be surprised. And if you're not taken by surprise, you and I will better deal with the losses that are inevitable as long as we are alive.

President John F Kennedy, when selecting high ranking officials in his administration, identified the weakness of each of his appointees, and strengths, of course, so he would not be surprised when they made a mistake. He all but knew what those mistakes would look like, was not surprised, was able to respond with more wisdom and less judgment, and ultimately recover from the mistake quickly.

Accepting that loss is part of my life, has made it possible for me to recover from losses and recover with renewed resiliency to be able to see the opportunities that life presents. After failed relationships and marriages, I met Marty, loved her well and spent nearly two decades with her. My own inner resiliency made it possible for me to keep trying after multiple failures.

Resistance to change is part of the human condition. And it is resistance to change that causes us so much trouble. It seems simple enough: change is constant and all around and inside us. So why the resistance? After working with organizations, mostly public ones, for 40 years, I have one central observation. When change happens as a consequence of an intentional decision on our part, resistance is minimized. When change happens as a consequence of someone else's decisions, resistance is often the first response. Except of course if it's a pay raise, though we can debate the amount!

Some losses are a result of our own actions, like divorce or investments that fail. Many that cause grief, however, are more likely to have happened *to* us rather than *because of* us. We don't 'cause' or choose cancer. We don't choose for our parents to pass away. The most recent recession was not something we chose, nor was the Covid-19 pandemic. As Stevie Nicks sings, "Dreams unwind, love's a state of mind." Dreams do unwind without being realized. A dream unmet is a loss. What dreams have you had that did not come true? If we are above ground sucking air, we will have losses.

Resistance comes following surprise, shock, resentment, or the age-old question—'Why me?' Of course, some change deserves resistance when it comes to erosion of human and civil rights. As you know by now, I'm really talking about the emotionally-based resistance to loss. Sadness is not resistance.

Denial is resistance. Anger, if held on too long, can become a form of resistance.

The first step in dealing with any loss is to acknowledge it, face it, feel the emotion it brings and start thinking about how to move forward.

I have a friend, a neighbor, Kurt, who is a good man to have at your side in a storm. Standing beside me one day, he unflinchingly spoke of Marty's love of life and her love for me, and how her passing was now reality. His calm, wise presence helped me so much in the midst of the grief.

Loss is inevitable. Grief is also inevitable. You and I can survive a loss, even a devastating one, if we have made peace with and accepted the impermanence of life, accepted that loss is as much a part of life as is love. If we have created an understanding with our loved ones about what happens after death, we will find our way back to happiness. The less surprised we are, the better we will be in the midst of our own storm. In time, we will find a way to thrive once again. Tapping into our reservoir of resilience to face life head-on, our own resistance to changes wrought by losses, can be minimized and managed.

How we leave things with our loved ones is part of having a compassionate death. A compassionate person can orchestrate a compassionate death, even if it is sudden. I cannot express the importance of the conversation that Marty and I had about what we would wish for each other after one of us passes.

Applying these insights into our personal lives may be harder than we think. Like you perhaps, I don't spend a lot of time—and don't want to—thinking about and anticipating loss. The idea is to spend a little effort and have a big impact. I am so glad that Marty and I spent that hour or two having 'the conversation.'

If you and your partner or family members can have that

conversation about life after the death of one of you, you both can be better prepared to live life fully, no matter what life brings your way.

One morning several months into the cancer experience, Marty laughed and said, "I thought you would be the first to go!" I said, "I know! I did too!" We laughed and hugged each other. We really do not know how or when we will pass. We can lovingly and intentionally have a compassionate talk about what we would want for each other when it happens.

CHAPTER 5, COUNSELOR'S RESPONSE

In this chapter: Even in the closest of relationships, we can't read each other's minds. We have to talk. That's especially so when it comes to what we want our loved ones to know, and what we'd like to know from them, concerning our wishes around death. Marv and Marty had discussed their wishes for each other. They each wanted the other one to know they could do whatever it took for them to be happy after the other one was gone. Without that discussion, each could only have guessed and worried whether they'd gotten right what the other person wished. There are so many things we cannot control around death, but we can shed light on a few aspects to help those closest to us.

Importance: For a person who is at the very end of their life it is important to let them know they have the freedom to leave this world whenever their body decides it is time to go. Assurance that you will survive and go on after their death frees them and also frees you to allow the next steps to happen. For the survivor, I've seen relief when the ill loved one tells their spouse to go on with their life—even seek other relationships, if it will lessen their loneliness and bring happiness. Though it can be an emotional discussion, it's important that a surviving spouse hears words of permission to seek whatever may bring contentment after such great loss. Ideally, it's best to do early when it's still possible to verbalize our wishes and give blessings to each other.

A grieving friend shared with me that his dying spouse told him she never wanted him to be intimate with any other woman following her death. Years after her death her words still paralyzed his efforts to establish a future relationship with anyone else. I can't stress enough that we need to have early, calm and meaningful conversations that free us and our loved ones to choose whatever may bring more hope in the future.

Clinical insights: Facing an end-of-life illness usually places us in medical offices, and it's there that you'll find brochures that can guide you through recording medical and personal preferences for end-of-life treatment. It's important to fill out one of these forms and to put it in an accessible place for family. One reason is that, if families have these written documents, they won't have to guess what they should do for you. Another reason is that doctors will have a legal document to support, and thus be able to honor, your wishes for or against medical interventions. In "Cancer and End-of-Life Care," Dr. Stuart Farber discusses balancing medical care treatments versus respecting and adhering to a patient's personal goals and values (which for most people involves being comfortable at home rather than dying in a sterile hospital where staff is attempting to extend their life). He recommends a clear discussion between a medical team, the patient, and their families to gain an understanding of the patient's wishes.

Suggestions: Facing a life-threatening illness creates a crucial question: "What do we want the end of our life to look like?" Most of us haven't really thought that through. Do you know what your loved one would say if asked that question? Can you explain what YOU may want that to look like for you?

One possible outline to help you with that important conversation is a form called "Five Wishes." It's a pamphlet, available in doctor's offices and in hospice and home health care offices and its simple outline makes talking easier. It's widely recognized as a helpful guide to families, doctors, and other involved professionals, allowing them to clearly know your wishes. You can fill out the document, check what signatures your state requires, and make copies for your family and health care providers. (It's considered a legal document in 37 states.) If you don't already have one, forms are available from: Aging with Dignity, PO Box 1661, Tallahassee, Florida 32302-1661, www.agingwithdignity.org, 1-888-594-7437.

CHAPTER 6

MYTHS AND REALITIES ABOUT RESILIENCY

My son Seth was 19 when we started climbing mountains together. For years I had been scaling mountains, mostly in Rocky Mountain National Park in Colorado. When we decided to start climbing together, we scoped out the possibilities and landed on ascending Colorado's 14,000-foot peaks—the 14'ers, as they are known. Because I was familiar with Long's Peak and on previous attempts had made it up to the famed Key Hole shelter at 13,000 feet, we decided to start there.

That became a fateful decision. Within our family, it is one that has become an important story of how we find within ourselves a strength that we do not necessarily know is there and how that discovery forever colors our life.

We started out at 2:00 a.m. We wanted to make it to the summit by noon so we could descend before the thunder and lightning storms that occur daily on the summit of 14ers.

We placed the requisite note on our truck dash, leaving our names, summit goal and time of departure, and walked out in the darkness of pre-morning onto the traditional route to Long

Peak's summit. Seth's strength, stamina and youth had him moving really fast while I had to struggle to stay with him! We had agreed he would lead as we hiked along following the light shed by our headlamps. As the sun began to throw soft brightness on the eastern slopes of Longs Peak, we doused our headlamps and followed the trail as it climbed up through the denseness of pines to the sparseness of scrub, then the bareness of boulders. We had used up much of our water by mid-morning when we crossed the Boulder Field and reached the Key Hole. The quickened pace of water consumption was primarily because of the blistering pace Seth had set. By this time, we were sweat-soaked and tired. The speed at which we hiked and climbed and the loss of hydration at the higher altitudes had exhausted us.

When we stopped at the Key Hole, we weren't sure we could continue. I was in pretty good condition, with only minor lung and breathing issues. Seth was really hurting. He was spent, dehydrated and had more significant breathing issues. He had never been anywhere close to this altitude or this depth of physical and psychological challenge.

We rested and let the sun's warmth resuscitate us for half an hour or so. Seth asked me what we should do next. I shared a description of the rest of the climb as I recalled it from the trail books we had studied: steep slopes past the Key Hole, and amazing views looking west along the ridge line behind Longs Peak. If we went further up the mountain we would circle behind the summit, then there would be rocky steep slopes, a tippy transition to the narrow and often icy, easterly ledges, and the final bouldering up to the summit. I told him that it would probably take us another hour and a half or so to reach the summit and that would be followed by the 4+ hour trek back to the car. We had time to get there but barely enough water to make it up and back down. I told Seth it was up to him whether we continued or turned back. I was good with it either way.

We sat in silence as Seth considered his choice. Some minutes later, he stood up, looked down at me and said, "What the hell, Dad, let's do this." He was determined to continue. What happened over the next several hours would change who he was forever and strengthen our bond.

As we left the Key Hole to complete the additional 1 ½ miles of the climb, we reminded ourselves that no matter our decisions, the mountain was always in charge and would determine if we would make it to the summit. We stayed glued to each other and true to Seth's decision to continue to the summit. We had to negotiate our way over black ice on the ledges to the summit trail, but we reached the peak in a little less than two hours. We were exhilarated. Seth was proud of himself, and I was proud of him. We basked for a few moments in what we had accomplished.

As if to remind us of who was really in charge, the mountain treated us to snow, sleet, hail, ice crystals and rain on the way back down. At dinner that evening, we each ordered two entrees.

The reservoir of resiliency my son found within himself that day on Longs Peak was there all along, but he didn't know it. He had not tapped into it up to that point in his life. But there it was when he had to deal with a challenge that he wasn't sure he could meet. His courage and determination were front and center, but it was his inborn resiliency that made it possible for him to accomplish his goal. It was my great honor to be there with him that day when he discovered what he was made of. That it was his decision to continue the climb, and not mine, changed our relationship.

Over the next dozen years or so, Seth and I would climb 22 of Colorado's 14ers. That first one proved to be the hardest, but the most important. From that day forward, Seth understood the strength he had within himself. He became an adult that day and led his father to the summit. This experience launched him as an adult. He was able to make his own way in the world and make solid, independent decisions. Those decisions included going to California at age 22, not knowing anyone, and creating a successful career producing late-night network comedy.

What I have learned from Seth's experience is that we all have an inborn reservoir of resiliency we can tap. We may not even know it is there until we need it. We don't often get to choose the circumstances or the losses that call on our reservoir of resiliency. Losing a loved one, a job, our health or family treasure happen in the course of life, but are not events we would choose.

My belief, fellow humans, is that your own reservoir of resiliency will be there when you need it. The simple act of remembering that this resource is there within you makes it that much more possible to face your losses and recover to live a full life.

DEFINING RESILIENCY

Communities can be resilient. That means they are able to respond to crisis or disaster and recover quickly and fully. That is, governments, schools, businesses and community organizations and families do what they have to do after a crisis to get back to operating normally. A good friend of mine, Mike Calderazzo, is a fire chief in Colorado. He tells me it is the role of a fire department to build a resilient community that can prevent emergencies, but also one that can respond to and recover quickly from disasters.

The same perspective applies to personal resiliency. We need to face our losses, recover and restore ourselves. Sometimes we can recover from a deep loss enough to restore our life to a level of function, thought and feeling that is equal to or better than the way we were prior to the event that caused our grief. This is a good goal. For me, I am that work in progress: I am trying to achieve a level of function equal to the time before Marty's passing. I may not be there yet, but I have gained something: I have experienced a restoration of my spirit that has more compassion for my fellow humans than before my loss.

THE RESILIENCY MYTHS

Let's dispense with some common misconceptions about resiliency after a difficult loss. These persist because they make others feel more comfortable being around our loss and grief; they enable avoidance of the hard work of transformation; and they are a reflection of the "self-reliant bootstrap" philosophy of life. Here's what resiliency is not:

Resiliency, or recovery, is not a matter of time by itself. Resiliency occurs in the context of time and takes time to build and to restore. But time alone does not do that for us. We have to do it ourselves, in the context of the time we have. Time alone does not heal our wounds. We heal ourselves consciously within the context of the time it takes. It requires a decision to face life with resiliency.

Resiliency is not a matter of toughness in the traditional sense or having a thick skin. Rather, it is more like the willow in the wind: We bend but we don't break. Toughness is redefined as the willingness to admit our pain, face it and carry it forward as we move to face life head-on. That toughness does not allow the pain to defeat us. That toughness is part of resiliency. However, the toughness that says I don't cry, I don't let it show, that sees tears as weakness, that kind of toughness is no match for the impermanence of life. As Kahlil Gibran told us in his classic "The

Prophet," the winds of change blow through our lives, creating holes in our soul. That is how we become fully human, knowing ourselves, willing to have the courage to face the losses in our life, including embracing our own emotions, and becoming more compassionate in the process.

Resiliency is not about keeping or propping up a positive attitude, which takes incredible amounts of energy better spent on healing. It's about feeling everything and integrating our losses as part of ourselves.

Resiliency is not about having enough "faith." My observation is that if God is only 'out there somewhere' it may make our job of building a resilient self that much more challenging. However, believing, seeing, experiencing God within us, as part of us, may be very helpful. Personally, I am comfortable imagining that God is in here with me, helping build my human capacity to survive and thrive after a loss, big or small. In the hours, days and weeks of quiet meditation following Marty's passing, I felt and still feel the Creator's energy within me. I can feel the Universe supporting me and bolstering my life energy, which in turn encourages me to live my life fully.

Resiliency is not a personality trait that you either have or don't. It's a decision followed by concrete actions. The decisions and actions are ones we make many times throughout our lives.

Resiliency is not about "snapping back" to life as it was. It's about letting loss transform you into something new. This is hard work. You will have to decide that you want to move forward. This came up for me a few different times following Marty's passing. Each time I faced the decision—do I want to go on living without her? And if I do, what does that look like? For me, personally, those were moments of intense grief as I faced my new reality, as well as moments of extraordinary clarity about the urge to move forward. And because of who I am, I knew that meant I would be living life flat out, to its fullest, if I did it at all.

Resiliency is not about denying how you really feel. That does not make us more resilient or 'tougher.' Having an open heart, however, to experience how we really feel taps into our own resiliency.

SEQUOIA TRUTH

Shortly after Marty's service, my son, now married with children of his own, came for another visit. Seth suggested that I come and stay with his family for a while, so we made it a father-son road trip from Colorado to Los Angeles, where he now lives. The two days in my sturdy truck were a salve on my soul. We talked about whatever came up for either of us—we created a safe place for ourselves.

During the visit at Seth's home, I took my first road trip without Marty sitting beside me. I kept looking over at the passenger seat, wondering how it was possible that she was not there. I drove to Sequoia National Park and Kings Canyon. As I got out of my truck in the parking lot, I wondered if I wanted to go on. It was one of those moments. As I walked into the trees, I opened my heart and asked the trees what they had to say to me.

It took only a few minutes to receive their message. Each of the trees had been burned in a fire. It may have been in the last five years, or the last five hundred, that fire had scarred each of them into their core. In a shape much like a teepee, their two-foot thick bark was burned away, revealing the blackened heart of the tree, while the bark ever so slowly was growing back.

Many of the trees are more than 2,000 years old and over 200 feet high. Each of them burned in a fire, each of them is still alive, still growing. I was living through a fire. They not so quietly told me that I could continue to live and grow even though I had been burned in the fire of love, loss and life. I did not know trees could be so vocal!

The message rippled through my body and my being. I found two Sequoias that had reached their great heights while standing not more than 18 inches apart. They became a symbol, for me, of what Marty and I had done in our life together. We had grown tall and strong together, each with our own strength, which we then lent to each other.

The Sequoia trees inspired me, helped me to heal and pumped a lot of resiliency into my reservoir that day. The source of inspiration can come from almost anywhere. Something, anything, that shows you the force of life in the world can be an inspiration. It can be another person, a bird in migration, whales birthing or breaching, a Haiku poem, the river flowing by on a cool spring morning, a sunrise or sunset. Any life form showing itself to you can inspire the life force within you.

CHAPTER 6, COUNSELOR'S RESPONSE

In this chapter: A great source of support in discovering our inner strength and qualities usually comes from other relationships in our life. In Marv's case, he found himself an encouraging presence as a father who helped his son search the depths of his resolve. He was privileged to witness his son take hold of an opportunity to test and prove his strength. Positive validation, for both men and women, is one foundational piece of resilience that, if it's been planted, remains within us. It's that "you can do it if you try" message that comes from mothers or fathers, or uncles or sisters, or a teacher from school, or in a professional relationship.

Importance: You may be wondering about your ability to 'find your footing' after suffering your loss. First, set aside the expectation that someday you will return to being the person you were before your loved ones' death. That's an unrealistic—really impossible —expectation. You may encounter the old idea, which still hangs on in our culture, that you'll return to some state of "normal." You may look the same in your mirror, but internally you are in an "altered state" after your loss.

Your world is also different. Losing someone infinitely precious to you, or someone with whom you've shared a significant amount of time, changes you forever. Give yourself permission to let go of pressure to go back to being the same person—living the same life you've always lived. Further down the road—someday—when you're ready for it, you will rediscover an abundance of energy as well as a purpose, bringing you a focus and a sense of motivation to continue living.

Meanwhile, and for as long as it takes, 'adapting' is what you are doing. Understanding that you are changed means your energy and focus will change. If it feels impossible to return to old patterns with the same familiar zeal of heart and mind, it may help to remember that your goal is not to go back but to get to know the new you. You need to adjust to things feeling very different while you try to look within—accessing your resilience to sustain you and assist you in learning about yourself.

If "starting over" is where we find ourselves after a loss, especially early in our grief, then discovery is what's ahead. Initially, there's the discovery of how to live without the presence of your loved one. That involves giving yourself permission to feel awkward, disoriented and just plain lost. It also requires you to realize it's okay to simply care for your most basic, primary needs. As you assimilate the truth that everything is different, and realize the resulting task is to discover who you are now, you'll be drawing on whatever resilience lies within you. It will be important to discover where and with whom you can find support while you discover what deep, enduring qualities exist in your heart and mind.

Clinical Insights: The parent-child relationship is the earliest and most common source of resilience-building material. After publishing *FatherLoss: How Sons of All Ages Come to Terms with the Deaths of Their Dads*, Neil Chethik was asked what was most striking about the seventy men he'd interviewed concerning the death of their fathers. He said it was the *intensity of their connection* to their fathers. "Even when a father had been dead for decades, sons spoke with passion, reverence, sadness, anger. It may seem that fathers and sons don't communicate much, but there's usually a tremendous depth of feeling between them," he wrote. "The father-son relationship may be closest to the mother-daughter bond. Children look to the same-sex parent for guidance and acceptance."

Suggestions: Perhaps you've experienced positive support from a parent or others. A wide swath of the population has had very little in the way of helpful, affirming relationships. There are also those who've grown up having endured much hardship that has fed their strength and resilience. Whatever your experience, it's valuable and affirming to look for and to look at your unique set of strengths seriously.

Is there someone in your life who let you know they valued you just because of who you are or someone who told you they admired a specific quality they saw in you? Recall who and what that is. If you need help remembering, consider asking a friend to help you recall situations when you rose to the occasion of actually accessing some of your inner qualities. Interaction with another person can help us find our strengths with the goal of recognizing what contributes to our resilience. We don't often think about our strengths, but it's uplifting to remind ourselves that we do have them.

CHAPTER 7

LOVING LIFE, FACING DEATH

My son and his family gave me the support I badly needed during Marty's illness and immediately following her passing. I spent several healing weeks with Seth and his family, in their home in Los Angeles. Being with my two wonderful granddaughters was the medicine I needed. My son and I were able to share our grief and our hopes for the future. It was the beginning of healing and restoration.

I was not yet sure I was ready, or if it was time to go back to my life in rural Colorado, but I felt compelled to start living the life that was now mine. I climbed back into the Chevy pickup that Seth and I had driven to Los Angeles three weeks earlier and headed east toward home.

My first stop was in Sedona, Arizona, to visit a dear friend, Sandi. Marty and I had known Sandi for 17 years, so this visit was a chance to lay a stone cairn in Marty's honor, say prayers for her and spend an evening together reminiscing.

As I headed north the next day toward the South Rim of the Grand Canyon, I was feeling more like myself. A visit with a friend had helped center me. I remember checking in on myself on the drive through the forests of northern Arizona and thinking that I was making progress, that I felt more secure moving forward than I had up to that point. I was excited about being at the Canyon again. I have always loved it there and seen the Canyon as a monument to nature's relentless forward momentum. I thought it would be a good reminder of my own need to move forward. Marty and I had been at the Canyon several years prior, so it felt like a sentimental detour on my way home.

I got to the South Rim mid-morning on a gorgeous day. The sun highlighted the incredibly beautiful rock and rim formations. I passed by the visitor's center and drove to one of the overlooks. I climbed over the rock wall and sat cross-legged, like I normally would, to breathe deeply and enjoy the view.

I had climbed mountains for fifteen years and hunted in the backcountry many times, so I was used to sitting on the edge of cliffs and overlooks. But suddenly I had the overwhelming urge to jump, to join Marty. The wave of desire—to fall into the Canyon—came over me suddenly and completely surprised me. It was the strongest urge I have ever experienced.

I had never had a suicidal thought in my life. I was stunned and overwhelmed by it. I couldn't move. Never, not once in all the 15 years of mountain and rock climbing had I gotten 'stuck' or 'frozen' and been unable to budge. It wasn't like me at all. But there I was, frozen cross-legged on a precipice overlooking a half-mile drop straight down into the Grand Canyon. I was certain that if I moved at all, I would jump. It was absolutely terrifying. I sat there for what may have been two minutes or could have been twenty. I slowed my breathing as much as I could, and that helped slow my mind and clear my head. If I had not done so, I would not be writing this to you today.

As my mind cleared, two thoughts coursed through me. One was that Marty would not want that for me; she would want me to live out my life. The second was that I had promised her I would be happy. In retrospect, I believe what was happening was that my mind, heart and spirit were suddenly overwhelmed by the loss and the pain of losing Marty.

Still, I could hardly breathe. I had to consciously inhale deeply and slowly, and exhale in just as measured a way. Finally, I was able to stand up and turn away from the edge. I took one step in the direction of the rock wall I had climbed earlier and then another till I was close to it. I hoisted myself up on the wall and faced back toward the Canyon. For a time, I held my head in both hands, simultaneously sweating and weeping, soaking my t-shirt.

I sat there on the rock wall looking out on the beauty and wonder of the Grand Canyon, stunned at what had just happened. I knew I needed help putting it into perspective. I got back into the truck and drove directly to the South Rim Visitor's Center and tried to call my son Seth, my long-time friend, Tam, or Carol, who had been Marty and mine's grief counselor and therapist. They were all away from their phones, but Carol called back a few minutes later.

She and I talked for an hour and a half. She helped me see that I had simply been overwhelmed—the pain of the loss was just too much, and missing Marty was just too much. What saved me was knowing how much Marty had loved me and how she wanted me to experience as much of life as possible—as did my inborn desire to do just that. My internal resiliency manifested itself in the ability to stand up, turn away from the edge and go on living.

Seth and Tam both made me promise that if I ever had that urge again, I would call them. Good family and friends do that.

The people in our lives make all the difference when we experience such intense pain.

In the moments when I turned away from the canyon and got up on my feet, I was not consciously thinking about being strong. But it was my innate resiliency that turned me around and kept me alive that day. In this way, our desire to live is a manifestation of resiliency. If not for the resiliency that lived within me, I would have died that day.

Leaving the Grand Canyon and continuing on the journey home, I made one more stop. This one was at Monument Valley. Marty and I had thought that we would visit there someday, but never made it. So, this was a sentimental journey: I would see it by myself, take her with me and let her see it through my eyes. That evening I was witness to one of the most beautiful and intensely orange, blue and black sunsets ever. I saw Marty in that sunset and thanked her for loving me so well that I wanted to keep on experiencing sunsets.

PREPARATION

As much as we have the resiliency to keep on living, we also have the resiliency to face our own death if we have to. If we are told that our death is imminent, we have the ability to face that too. Marty did so with uncommon courage.

She was never afraid of her own death. Her fear was that death would surprise her. She was fearful that she would not know it was near. She asked me to tell her as it got closer to her time.

From the beginning of our relationship, we made a commitment to share everything, hold nothing back. For 19 years we shared every day how much we loved each other, and we talked through the difficult stuff right away, without waiting for it to fester. During the cancer experience we also shared how grateful we were to be with each other and for the life we shared. We knew how fortunate we were, and I still believe now that I'm the luckiest man I know.

So that she would not be surprised, as Marty's life arced closer to its end, she and I would go over what her doctors and caregivers were saying was happening with her body. The nurses and caregivers were aware of her fear, offered helpful information along the way and we consulted them often during the last couple of months of her life.

Holding each other, through shared tears, we acknowledged in the last couple of weeks that her weakened condition made it obvious that her time was getting close. All of this was our way of dealing with and preparing for the loss of her life. We were fortunate to have the time we had to plan for her passing and for her not to be surprised by it.

Together we discovered that if you are not afraid of death, you don't have to be afraid of anything.

THE HUMAN HEART'S CAPACITY TO LOVE

The only limits on the human heart's capacity to love are those we place on it. Imagine with me for a moment that your heart has an unlimited capacity to love. It is not a zero-sum game. We can love our parents, children, spouses, friends, all at the same time. I equate our heart's capacity to love with our elastic ability to recover from loss. These are equal parts of human resiliency in the face of loss. Both are inherently limitless, though, as I'll discuss shortly, we place limits on both.

We see in our young children an unfettered ability to love. When I was in graduate school, I taught three-to five-year olds in a Montessori daycare center. I observed children forgiving each other with ease. They didn't talk about forgiveness—they just did it. They could love all of their classmates equally and with equanimity. It takes a lot of training for our children to unlearn this natural capacity to love themselves and others.

Our ability or willingness to love others is the same ability to find the resilience within ourselves to face our losses, go on with life and be happy again. Opening our heart is work we do within ourselves. We go to the same places within ourselves to tap our resiliency. The strength I found within me to back away from the cliff is the strength it takes to love life enough to survive its most painful moments.

And yet we sometimes limit our ability to love and to be resilient. Fear and prejudice are two dominant ways we do that. We may fear being emotionally hurt or rejected, of failing, of being loved, of facing conflict, of dying. We are really good at this. We have many ways to gin up fear, which in turn places limits on our resiliency, drains us of energy and diminishes our capacity to love life, others and ourselves.

Sometimes fear is rational. We could find ourselves standing between a grizzly sow and her cubs. Fear would then kick in our fight or flight instincts and that might help us survive. More often than not, though, we create fear within our own minds and without a real existential threat.

In my business life I often hear people my company works with say, 'What I'm afraid of is....' My take is that any time we—as individuals or as organizations—act out of fear, we are likely to make mistakes or miss opportunities, or both.

In addition to plain old fear, there is a laundry list of ways we place limits on our internal resources—our resiliency. Prejudices about others, for instance, can not only keep us from being decent human beings, but they can imperil our ability to get the help we need from others to prepare, move through and recover from losses.

The resources are within us and around us to get through just about any loss. It is important that we do not consciously set boundaries for ourselves by imposing restraints on our love and resiliency. Keeping our hearts open to other people creates a portal to healing.

Marty's skilled oncologist, Dr. Jesal Patel, is an Asian American whose background is different from Marty's and mine. Many times, he was there to extend her life according to her wishes. He was compassionate and honest every time we met with him. Many of her nurses in the hospital or oncology clinic were from foreign countries or born into cultures here at home that were different from ours. They and Marty touched each other's hearts and lives. Without those wonderful people, Marty's life would have been shorter and her quality of life much diminished. Limits we place on our ability to appreciate and love others can hurt us. They can diminish our resiliency and our ability to recover from loss.

CHAPTER 7, COUNSELOR'S RESPONSE

In this chapter: A discussion about suicidal thoughts and what to do about them is important in creating our ability to endure strong emotions that are a normal part of grief. As Marv described in his encounter with a surprising and potentially deadly thought, emotions can influence our behavior towards unhealthy outcomes.

Several points contributed to Marv being surprised by the thought of jumping and joining his deceased wife: He had never had such a thought before. It showed up when he thought he was adjusting well to life—It focused intensely on one, single idea—that of falling into the canyon--and it was, as he remembers, "the most powerful urge I had ever experienced!"

Is it possible to prepare for an occurrence that's as unexpected and potentially overwhelming as was this one? The answer is 'yes.'

Importance: Thoughts of ending it all—thoughts of suicide—are normal in the experience of grief. They usually come couched in a desire to "join the loved one" or to "end the pain of separation from them." Because they can become all-consuming, the power of our emotions should not be underestimated. Heightened feelings combine with random ideas that aim at a solution to stop our pain. It could be life-saving to think through the possibility of having an encounter with this combination of emotion and thought and place yourself on the offense by creating a plan to deal with it if it happens.

Clinical insights: When our emotions become intense, they can inhibit our ability to problem-solve responsibly. Our capacity to think of any number of solutions decreases. A smaller number of choices seems available than what really exist. As the emotion escalates, we can become focused on one single solution—one way out. We find ourselves struggling in a highly charged emotional state. Our access to self-regulation skills can be stifled by a more basic, primal, instinctual response that may feel as if it's in control.

Richard Pfeiffer, in his book, *Anger Management Workbook and Curriculum*, writes,

> "Emotions regulate and influence everything we think
> or do including our moods, our sympathetic/para-sympathetic autonomic balance, our beliefs, and our social
> relationships. If we are relaxed, wide open and accepting,

our emotions will naturally flow with our purpose of the moment. Emotion that is defensively repressed, *amplified*, or forbidden cannot easily flow back into a healthy rhythm of harmony and needs *firm internal guidance, or self-regulation.*"

Pfeiffer is referring primarily to shame and anger, but his descriptions and suggestions apply as well to facing the emotions of despair and hopelessness that are felt in the grief experience. He suggests developing the skill of recognizing the strong emotion as, "I'm being flooded with adrenaline," and that we help ourselves by saying, "This is a feeling. It's only a temporary feeling. Feelings are meant to be felt. That's why they are called feelings. I choose to breathe through this feeling, rather than act it out." Or to act on it!

Suggestions: Preparedness is key when it comes to surviving and thriving through our emotions in grief. Accept the possibility that your emotions may overwhelm you at some point. "Impulse Planning" refers to taking responsibility for any emotions you have that may create an emergency for you. You may consider yourself a calm, rational person, but the roller coaster of grief emotions can surprise you. Thinking through what to do if your emotions get the best of you can be life-saving.

So here is the plan—take the time now to make an index card to place in your wallet that contains the following items on one side of it:

- Slow my breathing: Count to 5 as you breathe in. Count longer as you breathe out.
- Distance myself from danger: Avert your eyes to a different location. Move your body away from danger.

- Place myself near another person: Go where there are people who can see you.
- Call friends: Write down the names and numbers of three good friends. Tell these friends ahead of time that you may call someday just to connect, and they only need to be a sounding board for you.
- Call The National Lifeline: 1-800-273-8255 (available 24/7)

On the other side of your index card write:
- Belly Breathing: Sit with one hand on your belly, the other hand on your chest. Breath in deeply through your nose counting to 5, letting your belly push your hand out. Your chest should not move. Breathe out as if whistling. Let your hand on your belly go in pushing out all the air and counting to 10. Do this 3 to 10 times. Take your time. Notice yourself relaxing.

CHAPTER 8

—————

RESILIENCY IS A
WAY OF LIVING

A lot of people treat resiliency as a kind of spare tire on the road trip through life. Much of the time it's packed away in the trunk, buried under layers of other stuff we might need someday. We rarely give it much thought but are comforted by knowing it's there should we need it. In other words, we figure we'll tap into it when something has gone very wrong, and we're stranded by the side of the road.

The truth is, resiliency is not a piece of emergency equipment we unpack only in times of stress. It is built into everything else we do the rest of the time.

In the 1970's, following the conflict in Southeast Asia, refugees from Cambodia, Vietnam and Laos arrived in the US with only the clothes on their back and a hope that they would be able to raise their families in a safe place and rebuild a future. During those years, I had the privilege and the opportunity to manage and lead the State of Iowa's Refugee Resettlement Initiative.

I was responsible for bringing refugee families to this country, all of whom had flown halfway around the world and who would arrive, sometimes in the dead of winter, at the Des Moines airport. The airport terminal became the modern version of Ellis Island.

Watching the faces of the family members already here, I could feel the tension as they watched each passenger deplane, anticipating that they would see their loved one walk off this flight. When their family member or friend or village neighbor appeared, tears of joy and relief streaked their cheeks (and mine) as they held each other in long embraces. Sometimes the tears became sobs of relief at being back together. Their emotions were a release of the sadness and fear built up over months, and sometimes years, of wondering if they would ever see each other again. Some, overcome by their emotions, would bend to the floor sitting against the wall, holding tight to an immediate family member who was thought to be dead.

Refugees coming to America from around the world have lost their centuries-old homelands, their nation of origin and all that was familiar to them. Hard to imagine, isn't it? It was plain to me, having the privilege to know so many of these brave new Americans, that unless you are a Native American, we are all 'boat people' from one place or another. Refugees who fled their homelands did so mostly out of a well-founded fear of death or persecution, simply because of who they were—their culture, religion, ethnicity and the like.

"Refugee" means loss. Most of the people I know from Southeast Asia lost immediate family members in the night crossings of the Mekong River, in attacks by pirates on the South China Sea or by insane genocide in countries like Cambodia.

At the time they came, they were the newest Americans. Now they are part of our society. I remember standing in courtrooms, feeling the hair rise on my neck and arms from an enormous sense of pride and wonder, watching the same people from those scenes in the airport be sworn in as U.S. citizens. Tears, this time of joy, were bookends to their arrival and their citizenship—and the years of hard work in between.

The refugees I know embody resiliency as a way of life. Their grief for the homelands and loved ones lost will span generations. Despite the sadness they may feel for what they lost, they never give up. Given the chance, parents insist that the children sit around the kitchen table studying after dinner each night. Those kids then become valedictorians, teachers and scholars, Olympic Champions, business and political leaders. Families and communities are building Buddhist temples, celebrating New Year's, and preparing feasts for newly-married children. This is the essence of rebuilding life after great loss.

I hope you are beginning to see that resiliency is not just a first aid kit for tough times, but rather is something we foster all the time in how we go about daily life. It is not a spare tire. It's how we drive the car.

But how, exactly, do we foster resiliency? Here are some ways that have worked for me to build my reservoir of resiliency.

RELATIONSHIPS FIRST

Prioritizing my primary relationship was key. I cannot emphasize this enough. Marty and I always said, "We are the deal. If we are okay, then everything is okay." We talked about how we created a third entity—our relationship, which did not exist before we met. Our relationship was our unique creation, born out of who we were and what we wanted. The relationship was our #1 priority. Virtually everything we did was intended to strengthen it. We had created the space within ourselves to 'hold' each other and whatever either of us was feeling

When we first decided to be a couple, Marty had asked one thing of me: to be happy. I said, "I can do that!" Within that commitment, Marty and I felt safe, secure and became experts on each other. We had what my wise relationship coach, Andrea Balboni of Lush Coaching, refers to as a 'couple bubble.' It was a space that only the two of us occupied. We connected with each other on all of our 'landings and launches.' Whether we were going to bed at night and getting up in the morning, or leaving for a business trip and arriving back home, we always connected eye-to-eye and face-to-face

In his book, *Wired for Love,* Stan Tatkin talks about the various ways people relate to each other. He speaks less about love and more about how we can create safety and security in our primary, intimate relationships. His book helped me to look back and better understand why Marty and I were so successfully happy together for so long. For our 19 years together, we made our relationship our top priority and were anchors for each other.

During the lifetime of our relationship, we faced a lot of ups and downs, including the stresses of being in business together for more than 19 years (and having to lay off our entire workforce during the recession), dealing with health issues and with difficult child custody questions and deaths in the family. These are the normal things that happen over the course of a long- term relationship.

Because we prioritized our relationship, Marty and I grew stronger, closer and more secure as the years went by. It feels odd to say, difficult to write and remember, but we were actually as ready as possible for the most difficult thing we could have never imagined: Marty's cancer and ultimately her death.

Don't do this alone

Beyond the strength of our personal relationship, getting and staying connected to our community was an essential element of sustaining my resilient self during and after loss.

Loss, especially when there is deep grief involved, is not something you need to do by yourself. I understand that some want to get through loss alone, but I've seen that even the most independent-minded Colorado rancher or Iowa farmer asks for help when coming up against a big loss. A friend, neighbor or pastor might be there to offer comfort. When the pain becomes greater than the desire to handle it alone, we all seek help and companionship.

The months Marty and I spent at home during our cancer experience were filled with friends, family, and caregivers who supported us throughout. When Bre, our wonderful caregiver, stayed with us for the last several weeks of Marty's life, she took over Marty's pain management and medical-related needs. That made it possible for me to just be Marty's husband. When friends Jenny and Matthew and their kids brought in dinner and good cheer, we gained the strength and stamina to sustain our constant attention for each other and our expressions of love to the end.

In the time since Marty passed, I have experienced the deepest downs when I felt alone. Isolation in the midst of a loss can cause loneliness, a loss of hope and even depression. Loneliness depletes our resiliency. Loneliness would have happily rented a room in my heart. Don't let it happen to you! Stay connected to your community.

Seek Counseling

Investing in myself through the grief counseling with Carol, now my co-author, helped me pay close attention to what I was feeling.

And that made it possible to release the feelings of sadness as they came up. Emotions common to the grief experience, such as sadness, anger, guilt or shame, can literally stick to us like blue dye on white cloth. For some, seeking out a counselor does not come naturally. Counseling can carry cultural baggage that comes along with the shaming of people with mental health issues. Either a good counselor, like Carol was for Marty and me, or staying in close touch with your community, is essential to surviving a loss and thriving in the aftermath. Remember the goal is to survive, ultimately thrive and fall back in love with life.

TAKE CARE OF YOUR BODY

In the days following Marty's passing, it felt to me as though she was torn from my body. I felt her being ripped from my cells. Science now supports that feeling with substantive research. The loss hurt so much physically that I could hardly stand the pain. My body felt like it had been run over by a cement truck. My tears flowed frequently, and my stomach would sometimes heave when I cried. I know that you know what that feels like. When we have lost a loved one, we often don't want to eat and may feel nauseated at times. Grief takes a terrific toll on your body. That part of my pain did subside, but it sure took its time, as it may for you.

Taking care of your body is a survival strategy. The stronger and better your physical condition, the more prepared you are for whatever comes your way. If our body is not in as good health as possible, we will undercut our ability to survive and thrive.

I know how difficult it is to take care of our physical self. Even though I have been an endurance athlete most of my life, I have had a difficult time getting back to exercise. I am still working on getting my body back to its pre-grief health.

TAKE CARE OF YOUR MIND

Our minds can seem to be in control of us. Zen Buddhism and other meditation practices teach us otherwise. Our bodies and minds are fully connected. We know that slowing our breathing is effective in dealing with anxiety and fear. What that means is that taking care of your mind is an essential part of taking care of yourself and building resiliency.

As our thoughts wander, so does our attention. Observe your thoughts. Try letting them go by without holding on or attaching feelings to them. See what you see and hear what you hear. In his book, *The Power of Now*, Eckhart Tolle asks the question, "Who is it that observes your thoughts?" It is important to know that you can observe your own thoughts. By doing so, you can look directly into your state of mind. After the loss, what are you thinking about? The past? The future?

Our 'monkey minds' are constantly generating thoughts. By paying attention to what is actually happening in the moment you can make decisions about how you want to think and how you want to view your situation. You can take charge and change your thoughts, if you wish. If you have the power to change yourself, you are indeed powerful. If not, well, there is work to be done.

Like so many going through the grief of the loss of a loved one, I, too, have felt sorry for myself at times. Do not let yourself spend too much time there! One of my Zen teachers taught that it is impossible to help someone who sees himself or herself as a victim. She was talking about adults who have a victim consciousness. This is a state of mind in which a person denies personal responsibility for how they feel and act, one where a person believes that the world is acting against them. If you find yourself feeling sorry for yourself and feel that, because of your loss, you are now a victim, I urge you to stop such thoughts. This will cripple your resilient self. You will be lost in the maze of self-pity. You won't be able to find your strength. Your ability to let go enough to move forward will be lost.

DO SOMETHING FOR SOMEONE

Through my journey with cancer and loss, I have become a volunteer for a local not-for-profit, Living Journeys, a group that is working with cancer patients and their families in our valley. I'm a better person for it. Helping others, especially those who have experienced losses similar to yours, is not only good for the people you are helping, it is also good for your soul. People who have experienced hunger and then work in the local food pantry have a deeper and different understanding of the people coming there for food than someone who has not known hunger.

Volunteering your time, being helpful to neighbors or work colleagues, puts your own losses in perspective. Everyone has experienced some form of loss and may be grieving right now, either silently or openly. Impermanence infuses loss into everyone's life. We can expect it, plan for it, and meet it with resiliency. Volunteering with our local cancer support organization and listening to others' experiences with cancer gave me perspective on my own experience and losses. I am not alone in this!

DISCOVER OR REDISCOVER YOUR PURPOSE IN LIFE

Over the months after Marty's passing, I realized that redefining my purpose was going to be important. My primary purpose for 19 years had been to be the best husband to Marty that I could possibly be. When that went away with her death, I experienced a fair amount of confusion and wondered about how to redefine my purpose. It was very much like answering the question, 'Who I am now?'

Rediscovering your purpose can give meaning to the rest of your life and your relationships going forward. This was hard work for me. I no longer had children at home who depended on me. My children were grown, gone and doing well. The things that I could do, like take care of my house, my finances, my business could have some importance, but were not enough to give purpose to my changed life. It was when I realized how I want to be in the world that my purpose became clear.

A year and a half after Marty died, I took a solo trip to Tanzania and stayed for a few days on the tiny island of Chole. At a resort there, I lived in a tree house for several days. Each evening, guests of the resort would gather around a communal table for dinner with the host. One evening, the conversation turned to the topic of living with purpose. Our host said she didn't know anyone who could actually say what their purpose was. You could have heard a mouse walk when she turned, looked directly at me and asked, "Marv, do you know what your purpose in life is?" By now I was able to answer that question. "Yes, I do," I said. "It's to live with an open heart."

My purpose continues to be to open my heart to life and to the people who are part of my life.

WE ALL ARE IN TRAINING

Surviving a big loss is tough, hard work. It is not usually a sprint, and it doesn't have to be a marathon. It can be more like a middle-distance run. Each race, each person's grief process, has its own pace, its own dynamic.

Remember who Glen Cunningham was? He was a Kansas runner who set a world record in the mile in 1934 at 4:06.8. He accomplished all of that while missing all of the toes on his left foot, which he lost when he was young and was burned in a tragic fire that took his brother's life. Cunningham's story is one of courage, determination, hard work and never seeing himself as a victim of his circumstance.

Running a mile, with all of its physical, mental and emotional demands, is similar to living through grief, except that the grief process has no discernible finish line. It never really comes to an end, any more than our love for those we have lost ever ends. It changes over time, and it changes us over time, hopefully in ways that push us to become more honest and compassionate.

CHAPTER 8, COUNSELOR'S RESPONSE

In this chapter: We can see how being aware of how other persons or cultures express emotions, particularly grief, enriches our own experience. Almost everything written about grief acknowledges that we all have unique styles of grieving and honoring our loved ones. But what does that mean, exactly, and what can these traditions do to support us when we are grieving?

Importance: As human beings, we are always attempting to create meaning from our experiences—meanings that are dependent on our culture and the norms of our country of origin, our family rituals, our religious practices, and our own individual circumstances. It's impossible to prescribe, to predict, or to expect any universal pattern or grief response to fit all people. In her book, *Grief: Normal, Complicated, Traumatic*, Linda Schupp explains, "healing from grief must be based on cultural relativism. What works for one cultural identity will not work for another."

As the refugees that Marv described left their homeland culture and relatives to venture into completely foreign, western surroundings they experienced a multitude of losses, and those were piled one on top of another. Their survival, in keeping with cultural values common in Asia, depended on the strength of the family and the community as a whole. We can contrast that value with western culture's elevation of individuality as a strength.

Clinical Insights: When teaching, counseling, or offering opportunities to share with those of Asian descent, it would likely be most effective to work with an entire family or group as one unit, rather than singling out individuals, even if there's one clearly identified person who displays great need. In Schupp's book, *Courtland Lee*, a multicultural counselor, takes note of the many ways different cultures approach emotional support: "In many parts of West Africa, healing specialists known as healers or sorcerers employ spiritual forces to help address a variety of physical and emotional issues. In many Islamic countries, piris and fakirs are religious leaders within the Moslem faith who use verses from the Koran to treat illness. Sufis are secular traditional healers in these same regions who use music to treat psychological distress. In Mexico, curranderas (female) and curranderos (male) traditional healers use herbalism and massage to alleviate mental and physical suffering."

Many cultures also consider psychological stress such as grief to be a spiritual problem. An underlying quality that must be present for any culture—ours included—is that there must be a trust in the power of the healer, the therapist, or the helper to understand your beliefs and your customs.

In *The Journey Through Grief and Loss*, Robert Zucker writes "...when I work with the bereaved, I'll often say, 'Teach me how you grieve.' Then, as their personal style of grief emerges, the work at hand becomes clearer."

Suggestions: We can become aware of our own styles of grieving by asking ourselves questions such as those Zucker raises in his book:

- Are we more comfortable with emotional expression or are we more stoic?
- Do religious or ethnic traditions influence our grieving?
- What have we learned about differences between male and female expressions of grief?
- Have we experienced disputes between family members or community about how we should grieve?
- Are we confident enough to express our grief in our own style, though that may differ from others?
- Are we more comfortable expressing feelings or processing our sadness through physical activity?

Knowing these answers will help us understand what we must do for own grieving and what to be aware of when helping others with theirs.

CHAPTER 9

CULTURE OF SILENCE

Many of us deny the central place loss and death have in our lives. We give them labels that objectify them and keep them far away from us. We have moved death and dying to hospitals, nursing homes and funeral homes, where professionals take over the process.

It hasn't always been like this. In the 1800s, grief was more than just an emotion. It was a way of life. Victorian etiquette put great social attention on public mourning rather than private grieving. There were 'mourning clothes' for adults and children, strict rules for widows and even jewelry fashioned from the hair of the deceased. Funeral preparation took place inside the family home instead of funeral homes—and for good reason. Determining that a person was actually dead was not simple; doctors didn't have the medical technology to determine true death. For three days following a person's death, the body was closely observed to make sure the person didn't wake from a deep sleep or illness—thus the term "wake" we use today for visiting or viewing the recently deceased.

During the early 1900s, funeral service practitioners transitioned from providing in-home services to establishing funeral homes where bodies were prepared for funeral services. It was during this time that parlors got a new name. They became known as "living rooms" since they were no longer used to display the dead, according to the National Museum of Funeral History.

Here we are in the 2000s. "In the United States, the end of life has become so medicalized that death is often viewed as a failure, rather than as an expected stage of life," writes <u>Anita Hannig</u>, a Brandeis University anthropologist who authors a blog on death and dying. She adds that "In order to break the silence that shapes contemporary American attitudes toward death, we must explore our own relationship to it."

Death and dying in the U.S. are uncomfortable topics of conversation. Instead of confronting their own mortality, many Americans tend to label such talk as "morbid" and try to stave it off as long as they can. The title of the graphic memoir by New Yorker cartoonist Roz Chast says it all: *Can't We Talk About Something More Pleasant?*

My experience is that the only way to live with a major loss is to face it head-on. To deny loss and death their rightful place in our lives leaves us without a way to incorporate them as an integral part of life, and therefore we abandon or avoid the ways to accept them.

LETTING GO

When we have experienced a loss, we often feel pressure and expectations about how we should behave. There is a sense that we should not share our grief with the community. Some of us are socialized to keep our feelings to ourselves. We can see the discomfort many people have when it comes to grief. We can sense it in their hesitancy or awkwardness.

When sad feelings come up, as they will inevitably during

grief, the question is, what do you do with them in that moment. When we feel like crying, that is our body, mind and heart telling us it is time to give ourselves over to our emotions. Not later—now. Being silent about sad feelings when you're grieving is a bad business.

I knew going into my own experience with grief that if I denied those feelings their expression, I would pay a steep price. On the day I sat beside the river and watched the geese fly over, I was experiencing the full force of my grief. But I realized that to go forward with life, I would have to express these feelings. Otherwise, they would generate physical and emotional discomfort that would grow into anxiety and depression. I was sure that was the impact of unexpressed feelings would have on me. It is no doubt different for others but knowing that about myself is why I made a commitment to talk about my sadness when those feelings came up.

FEARLESS GRIEF

A good friend of mine lost her mother to cancer over a decade ago. She faced her loss head-on and did the hard work of grieving her mom. Still, even today, she has moments when she misses her mom and sheds a tear. She has family members who avoided the feelings and sadness at the time her mother passed, and years later still have not grieved. It shows up in their inability to talk about their family member and what she meant to them.

My friend's approach to facing it head-on is what I call 'fearless grief.' Regardless of how others are handling it, how others may respond to tears, how long it takes or other social pressures, she fearlessly mourned the loss of her mother. It is not only okay but necessary and essential that we give ourselves permission to grieve and do so whenever those feelings come up.

Grieving Under Any Circumstance

For the first several months after Marty passed, I could not do my work as a consultant. Standing up in front of groups, working with them to facilitate cultural changes and modifications in their thought habits, was more than I could do. I could barely stay in front of the next breath I was going to take, let alone have the capacity to focus on others and help them find new direction.

After taking several months to recompose myself, I felt ready for my first customer—the city of Las Cruces, New Mexico, where the City Manager, Stewart Ed, was a friend who had known Marty and me for several years. He and his team welcomed me back to work and, with great compassion, gave me a soft landing. I managed the expectation of the department groups I was working with by telling them I may need to excuse myself if the sadness came up. On several occasions I had to leave the room and go outside. I would find space on a park bench or under a tree and cry. It usually took about half an hour for me to recompose myself. People were very understanding.

I did the same with friends and family. I told them not to be alarmed if I cried and not to feel they needed to help or fix me. I told them I just wanted them to be with me quietly and let me cry or talk. For new friends, I told them they might see me cry. This approach let everyone know what to expect and to create social and physical space for me to grieve.

When People Say and Do Really Stupid Things

On a sunny, windy morning in May, I was out at the cemetery for a quiet time at the gravesite, thinking of Marty, watering the flowers I have placed there in planters typical of colorful Mexican pottery. I was also cleaning the water stains from the smooth gravestone with a razor blade and soap. The cemetery is always a place to reflect quietly and communicate. Well, it almost always is.

This particular morning, a couple were filming themselves doing yoga in the grass at the cemetery. They were loud and changed clothing so that there were moments of nudity in between. On my way out of the cemetery, I drove by to tell them what they were doing was disrespectful to the people who come there to grieve. They were indignant. I asked how they might feel if it was their mother, wife or child who was buried there— would they act this way? The guy got very nasty. I got out of my truck and a very direct, close-quarters conversation ensued. They ended up leaving but not without hurling insults out their car windows.

Afterward, I asked myself: Is this our current state of affairs when it comes to respecting those who are grieving? I believe that too often it is. Ignorance breeds disrespect, and the less people understand or value the grief process, the more likely my experience that morning will be replicated. Perhaps this incident and others like it is a result of the culture of silence that surrounds death, and a part of the reason people are afraid to show their grief. This disrespect can be institutionalized as well, in employer policies that do not include grief as a legitimate reason for personal time off, health insurance policies that do not include grief counseling as a legitimate mental health service, or hospitals and labs that aggressively pursue the relatives of the deceased for payment after insurance has made payments. To be clear, not everyone is callous. Most of the medical providers related to Marty's care waived the fees after she died.

Reflecting a culture uncomfortable with death and dying, I have had some of the dumbest things said to me—not from malice, but from cultural discomfort and awkwardness. The usual "How are you doing?" can be so inane and yet puts the grieving person in a position of having to respond with something ridiculously brief and meaningless. My thought at the time was, if they really wanted to know, did they have three hours to hear how I was really doing? What most of us want is quiet understanding. Too often, instead, people want to fix us.

What I found was that often people project onto the grieving person their own issues, experiences or fears. Once, a well-meaning grocery store clerk at a local store I frequented came up to me and asked how I was doing. I said something inane, maybe "It's tough right now." He said, "I know how you must feel. I lost my dog last year."

It's remarks like that that kept me away from going out to dinner, walking down the street or going to the local grocery store for six months.

Here are a few of the examples of other non-helpful things people said:

- "Well, that house must feel big and empty."
- "I don't know how you can stay in the same house you lived in together."
- "I can't imagine the loneliness you must feel."
- "You must miss her terribly."
- "Aren't you lonely?"
- "Are you still in touch with Marty's children?" (I raised them.)
- "What's it like to lose someone so close?"
- "I hope Marty believed in Jesus."
- "I was hoping that when my parents heard about Marty, they would be more thankful for what they have."
- "Do you have regrets? I know I would."
- "What's it like when you go to the cemetery? I think I would be scared."
- "When my dad died, I was left feeling guilty and angry."

- "I wished that I had told my mom that I loved her."
- "You're so brave." (Yeah, like I was brave.)

More than a year and a half after Marty passed, I encountered a woman who had known us and knew that Marty had passed. She was an art gallery owner and going out to this showing was one of my first times of going out socially. She apparently didn't know what to say, so she asked, "How's your wife?" I said, "She's dead. She passed away in 2017." Now *that's* awkward. It was so odd, that later I laughed about it. But what is a grieving person supposed to do with that?

The worst of these experiences was heartbreaking. The evening of the day we held Marty's service, a group of friends and family were sitting on my deck. A neighbor, said, "We all should have known that Marty had cancer. We should have been able to get her to the right doctors. Heck, my dog knew she had cancer."

What am I supposed to do with that? To feel like I failed Marty? This person knew that Marty and I had spent half a year trying to find out what was wrong and nine months fighting the cancer with every resource we could find. I went inside and wept on my son's shoulder. I can still hear her say it, and it still hurts.

I'm sure those of you who are grieving join me in this wish: Friends, please consider what you are saying to someone who is grieving and how it might impact them. A very helpful piece of advice on this issue comes from Laura Scales, a wonderful grief counselor who graciously read this book and gave us great feedback. Laura suggests to her grieving clients that if they are going to make an assumption about people they encounter during the grieving process, make it positive and assume positive intent. It just feels better even though what they say may be ignorant, insensitive or uninformed. Good advice for keeping your heart safe when you are most vulnerable.

One of the coolest things that anyone did for my son and me after Marty's ceremony was to take us out fishing. Two close friends, Andy and Randy, are top local fishing guides. They took the day off and invited Seth and me out for a day on the water. They were so kind and thoughtful. Andy and his wife, Stormy, had been there for us throuhout Marty's illness and had spoken at Marty's service. They knew what we had been through and how we were feeling. They just let us be there with them: catching fish, providing company and giving us a way to experience some normalcy without expectations. That they did that still touches me deeply, and as I'm writing this it brings a tear of gratitude.

What do you do or say to someone who is grieving the loss of a loved one? My best advice is to say little. Carol and I talked about this quite a bit when my grief was intense and current. My fervent wish was that people would not try to fix me or help me feel differently. Just be with me. Just listen.

There are things that I appreciated people saying. Some of those are:

- "I can't imagine what you must be feeling, but I'm here anytime you want to talk or just hang out."
- "When you feel like it or are up to it, let's get a coffee." (or take a walk, or go for a drive.)
- "I just wanted to call and let you know I'm thinking about you."
- "You don't have to reach out, I'll stay in touch."
- "Can I stop by and drop off some dinner tonight?"
- "Just know we are thinking of you and the kids and will be here when you are ready to get together."

FIND YOUR GRIEF VOICE

Support organizations are literally created to provide what much of our culture tries to suppress: our voice in the midst of grief. Please, find the organization in your community that will give you a way and a place to express yourself.

My own local support organization, Living Journeys, provides services to all people who have been impacted by cancer in our Valley. Their services are similar to what most well-managed support organizations provide. These include support group meetings for those impacted by cancer—patients, families, caregivers, individual therapy, bereavement support groups for folks like me, youth activities for the children of parents with cancer, deliveries of prepared food. These organizations are designed to create a safe, confidential place where you can share your experience, show and articulate your feelings, receive support and understanding, and hear the stories of others.

CHAPTER 9, COUNSELOR'S RESPONSE

In this chapter: We can see how uncomfortable it is for people to talk about death and offer an appropriate response to a person who is grieving. Don't we all wonder and worry about what to say? Marv also shows us how an unfortunate response can be hurtful and can resonate well beyond the moment it took place.

Importance: It's just a matter of time before you'll find yourself facing a friend or acquaintance in an unplanned meeting at a grocery store or any of a dozen familiar places. At a time when you're struggling to manage your own feelings, it's especially difficult to know what to say or how to help someone else who encounters "the grieving you." The truth is the other person knows even less about what's helpful to say than you do. It does present a unique opportunity to educate someone else about what it is that helps you most. People want to communicate compassion and cheer up the sadness they're sure you must feel after your loss. The underlying purpose, of course, is that they want to make themselves comfortable by making you feel comfortable in an impossibly uncomfortable situation. It's the "What should I say?" moment.

The practice I highly recommend to any griever is to be prepared with a phrase or two to share during chance meetings. Choose a thought fitting for you and practice it until it flows easily, like "Please don't feel like you have to say anything. It's enough for me to see you care," or "Thanks for asking how I am. I'm having a hard time today but I'm working on that." You'll be glad to have prepared a thought beforehand which might put you both a little more at ease while you educate them that you're the one in charge of working through your grief.

My two favorite comments from acquaintances, who'd heard about the death of my brother, were, "I was sad to hear about your brother. I wish I'd had the chance to know him," and " I don't even know what to say. It must just hurt a lot." I responded that "I don't know what to say, either, but thank you for being brave enough to even talk to me." Acknowledging it's okay to not know what to say always seems helpful. It's easier to be on the offense with your comfortable phrase. Perhaps you'll even become more welcoming of unexpected friend sightings.

Clinical Insights: The discomfort with talking about death has innumerable contributing factors—for both the living and the dying. Here are some of the reasons family or friends may avoid talking about loss:

- Fear of saying the wrong thing and making matters worse
- Fear of loss
- Cure collusion with medical professionals. That is, refusing to face truth or pretending everything's all right
- Fear of what other relatives might say
- The notion that professionals know best, so nothing is addressed
- Fear of their own mortality
- Guilt/shame about what has happened in the past
- Difficulty facing the truth

Here are some of the reasons dying people won't talk about death:

- Fear of being a burden to family
- A lack of privacy (for conversations), especially in hospital wards
- Inner conflict and unfinished business
- Fractured, strife-ridden families
- Secrets that have never been shared
- Difficulty facing the truth
- Fear of upsetting relatives
- Never been a talker—don't want to start now
- Trusting the right person—a dying person may choose 'who' they want to talk to, and it might not be a relative, nurse or doctor.

Hospice organizations tell us that it's important to NOT PUSH someone to talk, but to make sure they know you are willing to listen if and when the time is right.

Suggestions: To become comfortable with a topic that affects 100 percent of us, we need time and space to talk about it. The intense emotional and psychological impacts that accompany illness and death can be more disorienting than we'd ever guess. The shock of how deeply and physiologically grief affects us can add to our confusion and fear. Some confusion can be alleviated if we take the time to understand what can happen and what our options are before we're in the midst of a death crisis.

There are significant attempts all around the world aimed at changing people's comfort levels about death. Hospice, Dying Matters, Death Cafes—hundreds of organizations—now exist to open discussions for anyone who wants to develop more awareness of death-related issues. There are different groups with ideas about how people of various cultures make end-of-life experiences a little less frightening. Our resistance to discussions can be changed to informed acceptance. We all need to practice and develop the skill of fearlessly listening to each other.

A gathering like "Death Cafe" (usually scheduled by nonprofit group) is a place where anyone can participate virtually or in person. It usually starts with 30 minutes of tea and "always cake" and follows with 30 minutes of discussion about experiences or fears related to death. Don't be surprised to find that discussions about death inevitably become a discussion about life. You can also locate illness-related (such as cancer) or hospice support groups. They tend to focus on specific losses and needs.

Chapter 10

Men and Grief

We named my dog Tippy for the black tip on the end of her tail. I was three years old when my dad brought her home in a little, car-parts box from our small-town Ford dealership. She was tiny, so cute, a black and white puppy less than a month old. She spent the first night in our house whining and scared. By the morning, her tail had started wagging and didn't stop for 18 years. I fell in love instantly.

My grandmother, bless her, had insisted that boys living in the country needed a dog. As far as I was concerned, she was right about that. Tippy's arrival is one of my earliest and best memories.

So was growing up with her. We ran everywhere together, or I rode my bike while she ran beside me. Together we delivered papers on my paper route, scooped snow, camped in the woods behind the house and hunted for rabbits and pheasants out in the fields. She was my best buddy.

I hope you have had companions in your life like Tippy was for me. She added so much love, companionship and affection (face-licking variety) throughout my childhood and adolescent years.

When she was close to dying, I came home from college to be there with her—she was 18 years old or 126 in dog years. When her failed health meant we had to put her down, I took her to the vet. My dad came with me.

I was heartbroken and cried as we left the vet's office. After getting in the car, my Dad told me to stop crying and suck it up. He reminded me that men don't cry. What I said to him is not repeatable here, but to say the least, I refused to be silenced. I refuse to be silent today.

This story carries a powerful message for me and for many men. It reveals how males are taught to deal with loss, as evidenced by my father's response to my grief, and probably his own. The message is clear: Men should be silent and hide feelings when a big loss has happened. This is how the culture of silence gets communicated from one generation to another.

The communication of culture happens in classrooms and at playgrounds, work, sports, church, and especially at home in families. Men are expected—and expect themselves to be 'strong,' that is, to not show emotion. This is a real mind-fuck. Men have the same emotions as women but know less about how to access them and what to do with them. This becomes especially problematic in the context of grief. When the emotions come, as they will, men often have a difficult time letting the feelings flow.

Antiquated notions of what it means to be a man (stoic, tough) make it difficult and complicated for men to grieve. The strong, silent type needs our compassion and understanding. When it comes to his own emotions, he may not even know how he feels or that he can talk it out instead of keeping it stuffed inside, or worse, acting out in a hostile way. A real danger for a man in this situation is that he can go through a loss and come out the other side less resilient and even more silent.

ACTION AND EXPRESSION

The generalized stereotype of males is that we deal with things through action—and that is often true. The stereotype of women is that they deal with things through expression of feelings—and that is often true. Stereotypes aside, each of us has to find our own way to deal with loss. I'm a mix of both emotional expression and taking action.

Some of the actions I have taken include holding a celebration of Marty's life and having our community participate, placing Marty's ashes in the grave myself, designing the gravestone, traveling solo, buying a new bed and moving from the house we lived in to a different one within my community. I cleared memories from the old house by burning sage, and I have placed family pictures including Marty's on the stairway walls in my new house. That way I see them every morning when I start my day. I also volunteer to help others experiencing the emotional overload that comes with a cancer diagnosis.

Writing this book is another action I have taken. But it is also an expression of my deepest reflections and feelings.

Some of the ways I have used to express my emotions include counseling with Carol for two years, writing poetry and talking with friends and family about how I feel. I have also found it helpful to meditate daily, spend time at the cemetery and observe important dates and anniversaries. I am keeping my heart open to life and remembering how well Marty loved me and how many experiences we had together that were wonderful, as well as the ones, like cancer, that were hard. I also attend and participate in cancer support and bereavement groups.

My experience is that it is natural and healthy to take healing actions, as well as access and express feelings. One without the other would not have worked for me. To act without knowing and expressing feelings would have left me stifled and probably depressed. To express feelings without taking action would have made it difficult to move my life forward.

Men, we don't have to be afraid of our emotions. They are a natural part of us. They can't hurt us or diminish us unless we lock them away. We don't have to be afraid of expressing them. Those messages we've gotten from our families, movies, TV that men don't cry—deny our true nature. We can be real men—badasses, if you wish—and be open to our emotions at the same time. Trust me, we can do two things at the same time. I hunt, fish, climb, hike, spit and swear. And I'm emotionally accessible to myself and to the people I'm close to.

The price of suppressing our emotions when we have lost someone close to us is much greater than allowing our emotions to be expressed. As I mentioned, if I suppressed my emotions as they came up, I would have ended up emotionally flat and a shadow of my true self.

Think about what the impact of suppressing your emotions is for you. The price may be steeper than any embarrassment you may feel in the moment when you let them show. If you need to keep them private, out of the sight of others, then do so. My advice on this is unwavering—let the emotions come and express them however and whenever you are comfortable, but do it. Let it happen. When I let the emotions go, they don't stick to me. I can keep moving forward a free man.

MASCULINITY GONE AWRY

A second danger for men who are grieving a loss comes when we do not have male friends we can talk to. This can place an enormous burden on the women in our life. In her 2019 Harpers' Bazaar article, "Men Have No Friends and Women Bear the

Burden" Melanie Hamlet identifies this as 'toxic masculinity.' She writes that "Unlike women, who are encouraged to foster deep platonic intimacy from a young age, American men—with their puffed-up chests, fist bumps, and awkward side hugs—grow up believing that they should not only behave like stoic robots in front of other men, but that women are the only people they are allowed to turn to for emotional support—if anyone at all."

In other words, a woman cannot be our therapist when she is our lover and life partner. She cannot be our only support and bear all of our pain. She can listen and be there for us, but it isn't fair to expect her to carry all our grief for us.

Similarly, mistaken versions of what it means to be a man create problems for both men and women. For me, men can and must be able to be emotionally accessible and tough at the same time. If someone hurt a female member of my family or one of my female friends, that guy would learn the meaning of sheer terror. I would make certain it would never happen again. My daughter's boyfriends in high school were afraid of me, and I wanted it that way. At the same time, I would like folks to think of me as one of the nicest guys they've ever met.

Here is why all this matters. If we are too tough to show or know our true feelings, we will not be able to manage those emotions when we have experienced a loss. Instead, they will manage us. When we allow what we've been told about what it means to be a man to define us and determine our thinking, we are vulnerable and at significant risk of not knowing what our authentic response is to a loss. If I don't know what I'm really feeling or why, that confusion will make it difficult for me to tap into my reservoir of resiliency and begin to recover. My confusion will stymie me.

When Marty died, my dominant emotion was sadness. If I

were still wondering what I should feel, I would not know how I feel. I would be wondering who I am, instead of restructuring and rebuilding my life. If I had not been able to name it and claim it, then I might still be struggling to figure it out. Instead, I knew what I was feeling, dealt with it head-on and allowed it to be expressed. Now I am moving forward with my life.

On the other hand, if we become an emasculated shadow of ourselves, then we wouldn't know what actions to take. The measures I took to grieve were essential expressions of my masculinity. That is not to say that what I did would work for someone else or that they would not work for a woman. They simply were actions I needed to take. As I've said, both emotional accessibility and taking action were essential to my grief process and to my ongoing healing.

Men Living with Open Hearts

Imagine if we raised our sons to know how they feel and give themselves permission to express those when they felt them. Imagine if we taught our sons to take positive action to show how we feel. Imagine if we raised our sons to know how to take care of themselves and do so not at someone else's expense.

Imagine if men had open hearts and full access to their own emotions when they experience a loss. Vulnerability is strength when it comes to grieving our losses. Access to our emotions would make us resilient even in the face of devastating loss because we could name, claim and leverage the knowledge of how we really feel to regain strength for ourselves and our families.

When I was asked on the trip to Tanzania about my life purpose, I said it was to live with an open heart. That was a year and a half after Marty died. I'm not suggesting that should be anyone's purpose besides my own, but I am suggesting we men could move a lot farther and a lot faster during times of loss if we open our hearts to ourselves and others.

Another benefit of opening our hearts is that we can become more compassionate human beings. Marty and I made commitments to be happy and to live with our hearts open with each other. That commitment made me a better husband, a more intelligent and patient one, able to hear her feelings, fears and hopes. By practicing that for 19 years, I was able when she was ill to hear her thoughts when she could not articulate them. I was able to hear her voice over what felt like the loud screams of my own emotional pain. With my heart open, I was able to learn from her how to live each day full of the simple joy of being alive.

CHAPTER 10, COUNSELOR'S RESPONSE

In this chapter: Grieving men, as well as women, search for a way to contain their sadness into a manageable form of expression. As Marv notes, many men run up against cultural barriers to expressions of grief.

Importance: Men's style of grieving tends to be quiet, but leans toward actions like building memorials or exercising. Women more easily verbalize emotions and cry. When asked which is more efficient, Neil Chethik, in his book *FatherLoss*, wrote that researchers found that "while the sexes grieve differently, neither gender does it more effectively than the other." He went on to acknowledge that we can make mistakes in our grieving, such as falling into substance or alcohol abuse. These could harm us, our relationships, and our careers, so we should take notice when we're stuck and seek professional help. Just having someone to talk with who is not a family member or friend can often break the logjam.

Clinical observations: A wonderful observation made by Thomas Golden (the author of *Swallowed by a Snake*) is that for all of us, and especially for men, the use of an object, a place, or an action tied to a clear association with the pain of loss provides a valuable coping tool, a container. The container Golden refers to "…is meant to describe anything that allows us to move from an ordinary state of awareness into the experience of pain, and then lets us move out of the pain again." We can pour our grief energy into the action, place or thing that we choose to facilitate processing our feelings. The idea of a container also provides the freedom for us to walk away from that process whenever we desire.

> "A man's action can serve as a healing container for grief if he forms a conscious link between the action and the loss. Each time he performs the action it activates the grieving process and moves it toward healing. The important aspects are that you do it consciously (do it intentionally, not let it happen to you), and that you in some way honor and acknowledge your grief in the process. Connecting the grief to one's activities has a similar effect as talking about it. They are both simply a means to experience the pain a bit at a time."—Thomas Golden

Golden offers several examples. One man worked every night on carving an image of his wife out of wood, thinking of her each time he approached the activity. Another man chose to write music. After Eric Clapton's four-year-old son died in an accident, Clapton wrote "Tears in Heaven," another example of a man linking his creativity to his grief. A different creative example is Abraham Lincoln, who suffered many personal losses during his years as President. He had a male friend come to the White House to sing what Lincoln called "sad songs." Lincoln would sit quietly and cry, thus using the creative element to connect with his grief.

Suggestions: An example of men finding an action, place, or thing to help them connect with their pain lies within this story of a Cree Indian named Jacque: When his brother died suddenly, Jacque was torn by sadness and anger. Following ancient custom, he went into the forest, selected a tree and, after uttering a prayer, stripped away a piece of the bark. Now the tree, like Jacque, had lost something whose loss caused deep pain. Many times over the following months, he returned to visit the tree. As the seasons passed, the wound in the tree healed. So did the wound in Jacque's heart. With the tree as a visible reflection of his loss, Jacque was reminded that he, too, was healing.

This Cree ritual, Golden reminds us in his book, "incorporates many elements...It provides an *action* in cutting the tree, a *thing* (the tree and its wound), and a *place* to visit to reconnect with our pain and healing. The power of this ritual is difficult to express through writing. I urge you to try it yourself and experience the healing that can follow."

CHAPTER 11

THE SCIENCE OF GRIEF

For me, the best analogy for grief has been that it comes in waves. The longstanding idea that grief comes in stages has not held true for me. That notion puts a structure on something that is organic, situational and highly individualized. In grief, we are as unique as individual snowflakes or the markings on giraffes—each of us experience it in our own way. We have experiences and emotions in common, but the people we lose, the relationships we have with them and the circumstances surrounding their passing is ours and no one else's.

I don't believe there is timeline for your grief, or mine. As a friend of mine said, it takes the time it takes. My timeframe to experience the things I have written about here is just mine. It may be similar to or different from yours. What is important is that we do not place expectations on ourselves for where we 'should' be at different points along the way.

The Greeks had a couple of concepts of time. 'Chronos' is time elapsing on the calendar or literally the 'sequence 'of time. 'Kairos' refers to the appropriate or opportune time for action or events, or literally 'opportunity.' Kairos is a helpful description of grief because we move through it experiencing a number of emotions and taking various actions when it is the right time for us. There is no template or application of Chronos to grief.

Expectations for how long grief takes or where you should be on someone else's timeline can only make you feel disappointed or, worse, a failure. I encourage you to let go of any expectations for how long you are taking to grieve or that you should be feeling a certain way at a certain point in the process. And don't let anyone lay those expectations on you either.

At this writing, it has been nearly five years since Marty and I got her cancer diagnosis, and over four since Marty passed. I no longer cry often, but there still are times when grief washes over me. It can happen when I'm at the river or the cemetery or when I see a picture or a video of Marty. I accept that the loss and the grief are part of me, just as my love for Marty will always be part of me. It does not prevent me from living and moving forward. It's just what it is.

A PHYSICAL EXPERIENCE

In the weeks and months following Marty's passing, I went through painful emotional, psychological and physical experiences. The physical included exhaustion, fatigue, loss of energy, loss of physical strength, headaches and body aches. I had episodes of shaking, loss of balance, weakness in the knees and wobbly walking. I felt empty inside. My heart literally hurt.

Grief is a very physical experience. For some of us, when we love someone, we become part of each other. When Dr. Ross told me that Marty had cancer and that it had metastasized in her brain, I felt sick. As I recounted in Chapter 3, the morning after we got Marty to Penrose Hospital in Colorado Springs, I needed to move our truck from the Emergency Room parking lot. I took the elevator down from the oncology floor. As I walked out the front entrance and around one of the wings of the hospital to get to the truck, I looked down and saw that my feet were attached to my legs and were moving, but I could not feel my feet touching the pavement. I could not feel my body.

When Marty died, I felt—and others have related similar sensations—that she was literally torn from my body, from deep within my cells. My entire being was in pain. Muscles, joints, bones—everything hurt for a while after she passed. I felt like I had been run over by a truck and then it backed up and ran over me again. When I shared this with Carol, she explained that this is what trauma feels like.

Writing about these experiences is not easy. They bring up sad and painful times. But I want to remember them. I want to acknowledge what it was like and what happened to me from beginning to end. I remember and feel what Marty and I went through together. Many of the stories continue to inspire me to go on and live a good and happy life. I find it healing to keep all of it consciously a part of me and to share it with you. Thank you for that.

MY RESILIENCY TOUR

In the days and weeks after Marty's death, I became consciously aware that my inner strength and energy were seriously depleted. I could feel the fatigue in my body, and I could see how slowly I was moving forward with my life. I didn't feel stuck. Rather, I felt like my energy had been completely consumed during the cancer experience. I was exhausted. And I carried that forward into the grief process.

While Marty was ill, I had become hyper-vigilant during the night. I could tell by her breathing that, even while she was sleeping, the pain was starting to come back. So I would get up, get her pain meds and wake her slightly so she would take them. That way, we would stay in front of the pain.

For months after Marty passed, I could not sleep for more than a couple of hours at a time. My nerves were raw. I could see that I needed to restore myself to stay physically healthy. I began to imagine how I might refill my reservoir. I had always been an explorer and a climber; I was a person who sought adventure. So, I decided to start traveling and put myself in places and situations I had never been before. I thought if I did that, I could begin to feel a part of the world again. I wanted to rediscover and restore my own resiliency by challenging myself and finding within myself the courage to face life without Marty.

This recognition that I was ready to do this came slowly. I recall standing in line at my favorite coffee shop in my hometown here in Colorado—several months after Marty died—and for the first time I spontaneously started to talk to a person I didn't know. Even as a very young child I would walk up to strangers and start a conversation. But during the early months of my grief, I stayed to myself. In that small, coffee-shop encounter, I saw I was being me for the first time since Marty passed. I thought maybe I was ready to reengage with life.

My first choice for solo travel was Australia and New Zealand. I had always wanted to go there and decided this was the time. From mid-December of 2017 to early January 2018, I put myself out there for one week in New South Wales, Australia, and for two weeks on the South Island of New Zealand. I felt a sense of security going to two places where English was the primary language and where Americans were welcome. Still, I put myself in places and situations where I had to reopen and extend myself to others.

Since I was putting myself out there to restore my inner

strength, I decided to call the trip 'My Resiliency Tour.' The trip itself was amazing. It included a 13-hour flight to Auckland and another three to Sydney. I walked all over Sydney visiting the National Gallery, other museums, and historic buildings that date back to England's early dominance of the continent. I went to a show and sat on the stage at the Sydney Opera House, prayed with Buddhist monks on the waterfront, viewed a Dutch Masters exhibit and another of Mapplethorpe's photography at the National Gallery. I people-watched for hours. An Uber driver I met invited me to brunch with her family on Sunday. I walked gorgeous beaches for hours and swam in their warm waters, exchanged my pocketknife for a boomerang with the wrangler on a sheep station, and talked sports in the local bars.

Traveling alone forced me to engage people wherever I was and whatever I was doing. Without a travel companion, your focus is more on the people you meet and the experiences you have with them. It was the perfect recipe for finding and putting myself in the world again.

New Zealand was a different experience in many ways. Kiwis, as you may know, drive on the "other side" of the road. When I rented the car to drive the coast of the South Island, I opened the door and got into the left side of the car, only to find myself looking at the glove box. I had to move over to my right to find the steering wheel and driver's side. I drove the coastline for two weeks, from Nelson westward, south past Greymouth, all the way to Te Anau and Doubtful Sound, around the Cape through Invercargill and north to Dunedin.

If you ask a New Zealander for directions, they are as likely as not to get in their car and lead you there. It is as though the country is stocked full of considerate people. They are outnumbered only by sheep, millions of sheep.

Every day I wrote reflections and experiences in my journal. There was something to inspire me at every stop. I saw abundant natural beauty everywhere. I would meet people at breakfast, rest stops, on the beaches, in the shops. I was still getting used to doing it alone but by the end of the first week in New Zealand, I felt mostly at home in the world again and on my own journey.

One particularly poignant stopover for me was at Greymouth, a beautiful town on the west coast, situated at the mouth of the Grey River. This is the same place where I was able to hear the rocks sing. The area is known for its jade and the world-renowned skills of the local carvers. I purchased a koru jade necklace, which is curled like an unfolding fern frond. For the Maori, the unfolding fern frond is a symbol of new beginnings. I was looking for a new beginning and was doing one at the same time. I still wear the necklace.

There is a spirit in New Zealand that lifted my spirits and restored my resiliency. It was almost a normal part of the experience to hike for an hour through a rain forest and emerge onto a wild beach where the only other beings are seals and sea lions. The day I hiked into an area reputed to have a remote and beautiful waterfall, I met fellow travelers from France. We climbed up a series of slick, flat rocks to see a breathtaking waterfall. I was at ease once again engaging people I didn't know. In New Zealand, I became comfortable doing it alone and enjoying it.

Captain Cook gave Doubtful Sound its English name in 1770 because it was difficult to find in the foggy mist that can cover the southwest part of the coastal waterways. The Maori word for Doubtful Sound is Patea. To get there, I first had to take a car from village of Te Anau to the shores of Lake Manapouri, a boat ride across that fresh-water lake, then a van drive through the mountains to the boat dock on the saltwater fiord of Doubtful Sound. For two days, I and the other travelers there explored the Sound with its incredible sea life, ferns and other plant life clinging to sharp granite peaks rising hundreds of feet out of the water. I especially missed Marty on that part of the trip; I knew how much she would have loved it.

I enjoyed the boat, the people, the wildlife, and especially Joel, the boat captain. He told me how it takes about 10 years to grow moss on the granite, how the first seeds to land and take root are the ferns, then larger and larger plants, all the way up to trees growing on the vertical cliffs. Every now and then there will be a 'slide,' when the plants get too heavy, break away and slide into the sea. A new ecosystem forms in the water below, with micro-organisms gathering around the new biomass. Small fish come around to feed on tiny organisms, then larger fish like Black Cod feed on the smaller fish, then dolphins and sharks come to feast on the fish. The process recreates an underwater ecosystem, and the entire food chain recreates itself in the sea.

On granite cliffs jutting up out of the sea, a tiny moss seed begins a forest, clinging to granite cliffs. Talk about resiliency! Here was a beautiful symbol for me to remember always. I had that seed inside me and could grow a forest of my own.

The cycle of life continuously refreshes itself in the natural world. As part of that world ourselves, our inborn inclination is to pursue life and continuously restore ourselves, even after we slide into the depths of despair following a profound loss. The natural world continues to inspire me to believe in our own resiliency.

Solo travel changed me physically, emotionally, spiritually and psychologically in many positive ways. It took me out of my surroundings, out of my comfort zone and away from my thought habits. It gave me a new perspective. It was a soft reset for the grief I was experiencing. At whatever time is right for you and with whatever experiences would work for you, I encourage giving yourself experiences that will give you that soft reset.

PAINT YOUR LIFE

On a recent visit to Santa Fe, I had a conversation with an acclaimed and accomplished painter and friend, Dominique Boisjoli. Dominique has a deep understanding of and well-lived perspective on life that she translates into her paintings. I share her outlook with you here because it has helped me put my grief experience into perspective.

Many of her paintings are sumptuous bouquets of flowers. She starts with a blank white canvas and an idea of what she wants to create. She begins adding layers of texture and color, one at a time, and creates her story within the beauty of the painting. She always leaves tiny parts of the canvas blank so you can see the first and then each subsequent layer of color. Each layer adds texture and color, and each subsequent layer adds depth and beauty as the picture and the story emerge. For Dominique paintings are like life. Each experience adds color, depth and texture to the canvas and remains part of us as we live out our life. Each experience paints the next part of our story.

Like Dominique's paintings, the layers of life's experiences add texture, color and character to who we are. Intentional memory is a way to leave each layered experience in place and available so that what we have learned remains accessible to us. All experiences, even losses, are opportunities to add character and self-knowledge to our canvas. Our reservoir of resiliency at the time of loss will have everything to do with how we traverse the experience and recover in strength.

Dominique's understanding of painting and of life resonates deeply with me. Every experience I have remains part of me and every new experience adds color, depth and texture. So now, this is my opportunity to intentionally paint the remaining layers that will be my life. Thank you, Dominique.

CHAPTER 11, COUNSELOR'S RESPONSE

In this chapter: Every aspect of our life and every part of our body can be affected by the sadness of grief. Emotional suffering, intense body sensations and psychological confusion are interrelated and can overwhelm us—even as each feeling ultimately has its own worthwhile purpose.

The variety of experiences which Marv describes while traveling, writing and interacting with people exposed different physical and emotional aspects of his grief. After he saw, understood, and addressed each of these aspects, he was able to blend what he had learned about himself and put it into a restored perspective of his life.

Importance: There is within grief the feeling that we live as if we're balancing on a tightrope. We're between pain, heartache and sadness stemming from our loss on one side and, on the other side, we feel the joy in the memories of our loved one and gratitude for having good friends. We may be mustering up on this other side just enough hope and happiness to care for ourselves and even have thoughts about the future. This balancing act is a picture of our new reality. We can have two feelings at once: sorrow and joy.

Clinical insights: Two out of three grieving adults experience a period of intense sadness for about six months —perhaps up to 12 —after losing a loved one. The deepest anguish gives way to a more moderate time of 'difficult' days and 'less difficult' days. Most do not develop physical or emotional complications. But some do. Grief can make them physically ill. Health complications can involve the brain and the heart as well as digestion, sleep patterns and daily habits. In 1835, Benjamin Rush, a physician who signed the Declaration of Independence, wrote, "Dissection of persons who have died of grief, show congestion in, and inflammation of the heart, with rupture of its auricles and ventricles."

Scientists and researchers, such as Dr. Selby Jacobs, Linda Schupp and Mary-Frances O'Connor, have published books documenting studies that show the physical effect of profound loss on the brain and heart. (There is such a thing as "a broken heart" caused by a disruption in the blood being pumped to one section of the heart. It can mimic a heart attack, but is usually treatable and temporary.) Further studies indicate that 40 percent of those who are bereaved suffer from major or minor depression and are at an increased risk for mortality from all causes, but especially suicide.

A pioneering grief theorist, Erich Lindemann, noted some seven decades ago: "What I experience changes me at a cellular level. Attachment, feeling secure, changes how I feel pain." This is like Marv's feeling as if his spouse was "torn from his body."

These altered or compromised behaviors or conditions brought on by grief are real; they are not the bereaved person's choice. This underlies why clinicians, family and friends need to be vigilant about providing support to those who are grieving.

In her book, *Grief, Normal, Complicated, Traumatic*, Linda Schupp lists some of the effects those who are grieving may experience:

Physical effects: "Headaches, nausea, appetite disturbances, shortness of breath, heart palpitations, chest pain, loss of motor skills, dizziness, insomnia, fatigue, choking sensation, muscle weakness, dry mouth, empty or fluttering sensations in the stomach."

Emotional effects: "Sorrow, fear, anxiety, guilt, anger, relief, numbness, release, helplessness, listlessness, loneliness, longing."

Cognitive effects: "Memory problems, inability to concentrate, problems with decision making, confusion, auditory or visual hallucinations."

Behavioral effects: "Wearing clothing of deceased, crying, keeping room of deceased intact, carrying picture or object of deceased, absentmindedness, distancing from people."

Robert Neimeyer, a grief theorist and researcher, notes that every feeling or emotion that one may go through while grieving has a function or a purpose. Schupp's book lists some of those functions:

Denial*, anesthetizes us to buy time for gradual comprehension of our loss, making it bearable; [see note below]

Anger / hostility, acts as a self-defense emotion, demanding life operate according to our expectations

Guilt, exposes our culpability, self appraises our competence and how we let the loss occur

Anxiety, awakens awareness of our inability to control events or to prevent or predict this loss

Depression, causes us to withdraw allowing for inward self-reflection about what has happened

---

* Denial is an outdated term that has been replaced by descriptions of a state of non-reality.

Fear, alarms survivors of major changes in their assumptions about themselves and others."

In addition to all of these effects, there is the experience of *forgetfulness*, especially in the early days following a death. Keys or glasses are misplaced, names may be forgotten, phone numbers and codes to garage door openers are hard to remember. Forgetfulness is part of normal distracted lives and part of aging, but dysfunctional confusion can set in when the emotional state is severely disrupted. Normal activities may take more concentration and energy. A reminder to someone who has experienced the loss of a loved one: You're not losing your mind, you're grieving!

Suggestions: Although physical complications are considered normal to the grief experience, when they extend beyond our personal ability to manage them well, it's wise to meet with a grief counselor, set up a periodic check-up with your doctor, and locate a good support group to meet others going through similar difficulties.

Take notice of anything in your body that feels out of the ordinary. It may be part of your unique response to the disruptive intensity of your loss. When we recognize the source of the feeling and determine what the sensation may be showing us about ourselves, we can then act. An action may consist of processing out loud what is happening with another person or of choosing an activity, like a walk or a workout session, to help alleviate the sensation.

The course of healthy grieving is built into our genes; growing from losses is such a natural process that much of it will happen without our direction. That said, the basic tasks you face include acknowledging the reality of your loss and expressing all of your feelings about it; learning to adjust to life without your loved one;

discovering an inner peace with your loss.

This is your work. This is the journey you are on. Practice listening to your heart and your body. And keep in mind that, as the helpful folks at Good Therapy remind us, "What gets thrown out of whack during the grieving process can, in fact, get back on track."

CHAPTER 12

GETTING OUT OF
YOUR OWN WAY

As I was grieving the loss of Marty, I would often feel helpless in the face of really big waves of grief, especially early on. I isolated myself—I could not face being in public—and I allowed myself to feel lonely. I felt sorry for myself. I felt bad that I could not have done more for Marty.

All of these things were a natural part of grieving over a loss. Eventually, they passed. But what I would like to focus on here is getting out of your own way and allowing others to help you through your grief and to a point where you can reconstruct your life.

Help can come in many forms. Sometimes it is simply accepting the grace that others bestow. For a year or more, the owners of my favorite local restaurants would not let me buy my own drinks. Members of my community reached out to invite me to their homes or to take me along on hunts or long walks. Friends and acquaintances reached out with hugs and affection. Some of them would sit with me, let me cry and reminisce. Relatives called out of the blue to check in and provide respite and refuge from the aloneness.

These acts of kindness from people within my community of friends and family touch me still. But help can also come from strangers. I would like to share two stories from a trek I took to Nepal some 20 years ago. There were two instances on that trip where my life depended on the help of others. I internalized important lessons from those experiences that have helped me make my way through the loss of Marty and the ensuing grief.

CHO LA PASS

In 2000, I went on a Himalayan trekking and climbing trip. Before I went, I spent a decade training stateside. My son and I climbed 22 of Colorado's 14,000 ft. peaks. I hiked and scaled hills and mountains whenever possible. On business trips, I ran up and down the hotel stairs with a heavy pack. I had no idea how hard it might be to ascend a mountain in Nepal or what I might experience at high altitudes, but I had dreamt of climbing in the Himalayas since I was a young man.

When I arrived in the Himalayas, four of us—two Sherpas, the expedition company owner and I—spent four weeks above 15,500 ft. We summited one peak at 18,300 ft and four more peaks at 17,800 ft, and we made it to Mount Everest Base Camp. But more meaningful than the physical climb was what I learned from the Buddhist Sherpas. They looked inside themselves for happiness. Material wealth meant virtually nothing to them. Social success as we define it in the West meant nothing.

At one point on the trek, we stopped at the Tengboche Monastery. There, a 100-year-old Buddhist monk taught me to be thankful each morning that I had awakened to another day, and to go to sleep at night thankful for the blessing of the day. I have adopted his teachings of gratitude into my life.

A few days later, we traversed the Chola Pass. It was there that I was forced to question my assumptions about how strong and how tough I was. In doing so, I found a resiliency within myself that I had only hoped was there. I surely needed it.

We had stayed the night before with a couple who were yak herders. They lived in a small house, which was part of a pasture where they kept four big, black yaks. The house was made of stacked rocks with yak dung as the mortar that held the walls together. There was a simple door, no chimney and the only cooking facility was three stones sticking out of the dirt floor where the woman had a pot of water boiling over a fire.

Without a chimney, the smoke from the fire hung about three feet off the floor. We had to lay down and prop ourselves up on an elbow to stay below the smoke. These folks were living the same as the Sherpas would have in the 14th century. It was my 50th birthday, and it was a gift to have food and shelter for the night. During the night, I reached for the flashlight to go outside to relieve myself. When I did, I stuck my hand into a pile of fresh yak dung. Another birthday present!

The next morning, we struck out for the steep slopes of the Chola Pass, which would lead us into the Everest Valley. Our first problem: The water the yak couple had packed for us was too contaminated by smoke to be drinkable. Then, the Pass was unexpectedly icy and treacherous. We should have been roped up and wearing crampons for grip, but no one expected winter conditions in May. Several times during the climb, Phorba, the climbing Sherpa on the trek, reached down with an ice axe to pull me up over ice and rock. Several times, the trek leader, Gary, placed his foot behind mine to prevent me from slipping and falling several hundred feet. Six hours later, we reached the top and were enveloped in a blizzard. Another surprise in May.

After topping out the pass, there was another May surprise: snow covered the field we had to cross. We post-holed our way across the deep snowfield. Post-holing, as you may know, is when you sink up to your crotch in snow with every step. Beyond the snowfield, we continued several miles on a trail that took us onto a glacier that was shifting treacherously. Ahead was a teahouse—one of many small bed-and-breakfast like outposts that exist along popular trekking trails. It was supposed to be our landing place for that night, only no one was there when we arrived. We had trekked and climbed for 15 hours without water, but we had to keep going to another rest stop. It was the longest day of my life.

This was the most treacherous climb I have ever been on. I was humbled by the simple assistance the Sherpa and my guide offered and by what it took to survive it. I had found resiliency within myself to keep going but I had to accept that I had needed their occasional assistance.

SICKNESS IN THE KHUMBU

Later in the trek, I had another experience that I would not have survived without the help of others. I became deathly ill.

Sherpa people live in small villages and single dwellings scattered throughout the Everest Region. We were trekking in an area known as the Khumbu. Sherpa homes are a place to stay in the Khumba; they make it possible to trek from one place to another. This style of travel, often called tea house trekking, is a little like staying in bed and breakfasts in a European country like Ireland, except that travel is by foot, not car, and the accommodations, while welcoming, are very basic. Water is brought from a stream and boiled. No meat is served. (Sherpas are Buddhist and do not believe in killing.) The primary food dish in the Khumbu is Dal

Bhat, a highly nutritious, soup-like combination of steamed rice and lentils.

Even though I was high up at 15,500 feet for nearly four weeks, I was very fortunate not to experience any severe altitude sickness, which makes many travelers to the region miserable and sends many home. Some trekkers and climbers are also afflicted by the 'Khumbu cough,' a hacking cough prompted by very low humidity at very high altitude.

One has to drink as much water as possible to stave off altitude sickness or the cough. Water is literally the source of life in the Himalayas.

Sherpa homes vary from wood structures to cement-mortared stone, or like the yak herders, loose stones held together with yak-dung as mortar. The beds for trekkers are padded benches along the inner walls of the house. Most Sherpa teahouses, which are actually family homes, are very welcoming and comfortable.

We were now near the end of the trek and the plan was to stay in Namche Bazaar, the capital of the Khumbu, for a couple of days of rest. Then we would make our way to Lukla, where we would catch a plane back to Kathmandu.

By the way, if you survive the flights in and out of Lukla, you can survive just about anything. If you're on an airplane that's landing in Lukla, you see a runway that starts at the edge of a very high cliff and runs uphill, which fortunately slows the plane down. Taking off, well, you just run out of airstrip on the cliff and hope the plane has enough oomph to pull itself up. I saw more than one traveler reach for the barf bag.

On our way out of the Khumbu, we stopped overnight at one of the Sherpa teahouses a couple of days out from Namche. We had Dal Bhat for breakfast. Possibly the water for making the dish was not fully boiled. Whatever it was, I began to feel sick as we made our way to the next stop, the Sherpa home of Pimba, a friend of one of the Sherpas. By afternoon I started retching and was very, very sick.

I was lucky to be at Pimba's when it happened. Lakpa, his adult daughter, cared for me tirelessly. She made sure I drank water after every vomit to keep me from becoming dehydrated and passing out. I can remember still the feel of her hand supporting the back of my head, lifting me to take a drink of water. I would sweat, chill, retch, drink, rest, and start it all over again every 10 to 15 minutes for the next 36 hours. I wasn't sure if I was going to survive. I even pulled myself up on one elbow, looked up at my companions and asked, "Am I going to die?" The response was, "Man, I don't know."

That was when my hosts and companions started talking seriously about whether or not I was going to make it out of this alive. I could hear Pimba, Lakpa and my colleagues huddled in the kitchen discussing what to do. They believed it was a make-or-break situation and wanted to give me an herb the Sherpa call pongmor, which is harvested as a round-shaped seed. That evening they explained that swallowing it would either take the poison out of me or if it didn't, well then, I could start saying my goodbyes because nothing was going to help me. I took it with the next drink of water.

I'm here to say that it worked. After another day and a half of resting, drinking water and eating lots of good Sherpa Dal Bhat, I was dancing with Lakpa in the kitchen.

We had been on the trek for four weeks when I got sick. I was in the best physical condition of my adult life, the condition climbers call mountain strong. I was as lean and physically well as I could possibly have been when I became ill. I survived only because of the kindness, generosity and special knowledge of a

Sherpa family living in rural Nepal.

Resiliency, the ability to survive and then thrive once again, often comes by way of the care and energy people give us in our greatest time of vulnerability. This is what I mean when I encourage you to get out of your own way, to let go of pride, stubbornness, guilt, shame and anything else that stands in the way of letting others help you.

My life was very nearly lost those days at Pimba's house. If that had happened, Marty and I would not have married—we were already in a relationship—or had those 19 wonderful years together.

What I learned is that when you are at your most vulnerable, set your ego aside and allow people who want to help be there for you. We don't have to grieve alone. To replenish our reservoir of resiliency, we need to let others come close and help us through this.

The trip to Nepal jump-started my journey toward Buddhism, my search to find out more about who I am and what I am made of. This search for meaning brought an unexpected bonus: the discovery of resiliency. I had a strong sense of purpose for myself and for the trip. That sense of purpose, my years of training, two very capable Sherpa friends and an expedition leader, made it possible for me to survive the day on Chola Pass and the sickness at Pimba's house. Resiliency is something we can foster, train into ourselves, and build into our capacity to face things we cannot foresee.

When I came home to Marty five weeks later and 10 pounds lighter, I was a better, different man. I was ready to love her with all my heart. And I knew much more about my heart than when I left.

LETTING GRIEF HAVE ITS WAY

The hardest and most important thing I've discovered is to allow grief to happen. Getting out of my own way to let the feelings flow was perhaps the most consequential thing I learned as I grieved. I cannot express this strongly enough. Whatever those feelings related to a loss are, do NOT stop, divert, delay, deny or ignore them!

I realize this is not the first or only time I've addressed this in the book. There's a reason why. It is essential to who we are as humans and to our ability to call on our inner strengths.

To me, grief is like a lover—letting her have her way with me so I can truly allow myself to feel, be fully alive, be fully human and heal. You trust it. You go with it when it comes up. When the feelings come, embrace them. Then you can come back to yourself and your life.

Many of us suppress those feelings for a number of reasons: It's too painful or it's not convenient right now. We might feel we'll be embarrassed to cry and that the people we're with won't care or understand and then we'll have to explain ourselves and we don't want to talk about it. You can often feel those strong emotions coming on and have time to make a decision: Either ignore or suppress them or let them get expressed at the time they come up.

There is a sense of immediacy or urgency to those feelings; they seem to need to be expressed at the time they come up. If I tried to recover the feelings later, it was more of an intellectual effort.

Whatever those feelings are at a given moment, they are what your psyche, spirit and mind are trying to express. Our deeper wisdom is telling us how we feel, how we are experiencing our incredible loss and giving us the chance to ease the hurt within us.

Expressing your feelings as they come up is a way to be present and live authentically in the moment. It was very important to me to live honestly and avoid any sense that others might not understand. I knew they couldn't really comprehend what I had experienced. Being authentic and honest about how you are really feeling gives others an opportunity to grapple with what you are experiencing. Without that, they can't be truly supportive.

I was very fortunate not to have my grief experience complicated by guilt, shame, anger or regrets.

Everyone experiences loss. It comes along with life. Loss of dreams and ideals, of a job or opportunity, of self-esteem when we don't live up to our own standards. It can be a long list for some of us. We face the loss of our own life and there is the loss of loved ones, which will happen if we live long enough. The more we love, the more we have to lose. Love and loss are in nearly equal proportion. Embracing loss as part of life leads to a rich, deeply fulfilling encounter with our own existence.

The central idea of this book is to inspire and encourage us to embrace our losses as an essential part of living a full life. I say this in the face of losing the love of my life, my wife of 19 years. Friends have said that this is a courageous position to take. Honestly, it is the only one I can take. I would not survive if I tried to hide from or avoid the grief. It is the only way I know to move forward to again live life fully.

CHAPTER 12, COUNSELOR'S RESPONSE

In this chapter: Often, when we're in distress, we don't take the time to ask ourselves what we actually need or want, other than to stop the pain. There are some needs we experience within grief that we're able to take care of for ourselves, and others we're unable to address at all. We need help with some situations we encounter. Marv described his limited ability to take care of himself during a mountain climb and to an even greater extent when an illness overcame him while climbing. His need was for his climbing buddies to help him find medicine and help him survive his distressing sickness. He could have refused their offers of care, but it proved lifesaving for him to allow their intervention.

Importance: We also require the support of friends when our processing mechanisms overload and our sadness overwhelms us. It may go against our own self-sufficient individualism, or maybe our pride, to ask for help—but, because grieving the death of a loved one is the hardest work we'll ever do, we can lessen our burden by allowing others to be there for us. We seem to be built more for community than for isolation. It's important for us to find a connection with other people. It also gives others the opportunity to assist us, and most of our friends appreciate the chance to feel helpful and needed.

Clinical insights: Therapists and grief advocates who have written extensively about dealing with grief note that although the initial tendency may be to withdraw from people, "drawing on the experiences and encouragement of friends, fellow grievers, or professional counselors, is not a weakness but a healthy human need. And because mourning is a process that takes place over time, this support must be available months and even years after the death of someone in your life."—Alan Wolfelt, *Understanding Your Grief.*

"Companionship, reflection and connection are vital parts of surviving grief. Many grieving people feel like they're on another planet or wish they could go to one. We all need a place where we can share what's really going on, without feeling corrected or talked out of anything. While some friends and family can do this well, I've found that it's the community of fellow grievers that understands this best."—Megan Devine, *It's OK That You're Not OK*.

"Finding others who have shared a similar depth of pain lets you know that everything you're experiencing is normal, even if seemingly bizarre. Finding others who live inside this territory of grief validates the nightmare of what you already know: there are things that can never 'get better.' That may seem like the opposite of helping, but for those experiencing deep loss, having others recognize the depths of the pain is lifesaving. Companionship inside loss is one of the best indicators, not of "recovery," but of survival. Survival can be forged on your own, certainly, but it's so much easier when you travel with a wider tribe of grieving hearts."— Megan Devine, *It's OK That You're Not OK*.

Suggestions: Even if you think it is impossible, consider being found by your tribe of grieving hearts. You will want to look for people who allow you to openly express your feelings, without judgment or advice-giving, and avoid people who try to take your grief away from you, or who try to fix you.

Go on a hunt for your "tribe" by searching for a grief support group in your city, online, at your library or local church. You can also call a nearby Hospice—there are many. It takes courage to approach something new, but you may discover you feel most comfortable with others who understand your grief. You need the support of people who value and honor your loss.

Picture the description of Marv's Sherpa guide placing his foot behind Marv's foot as they ascended an icy mountain wall, in order to prevent Marv's sliding off the mountain. There are friends who will do that for you—who will be there to support you and prevent your sliding off the mountain into despair. Your assignment is to go on a search for those kind souls.

CHAPTER 13

A TOXIC TRIO

Doubt, guilt and regret are a toxic trio that can keep us from moving forward after a loss. I am bringing you along with me on this part of the journey to highlight my own struggle and what I've seen others do to handle—or not—the trio.

I faced doubt immediately following Marty's passing, and revisited it even as I grieved. I questioned my ability to cope with the loss, to help my children deal with it and to see that life could be good again. I was very fortunate not to also have to deal with guilt or regrets.

GUILT AND REGRETS

If we do not face losses directly and acknowledge and honor the grief that comes with loss, then the loss sits inside us. That is, the emotions stick to us if we don't deal with them. Unresolved grief can come up and out in many ways, from seemingly inexplicable anger, impatience or frustration to troubled relationships. This was true in my family of origin and is not uncommon for many of us.

'Un-grieved' losses build up in us and make it that much more difficult to handle the next loss. They lurk in the background without us knowing they are there. But the accumulation of unaddressed losses can make it more difficult to face the next trauma. I found this to be true when Marty died. I was dealing with the loss of her, and with old losses as well.

I have seen this happen to others in a deep and destructive way. Years ago, while attending graduate school, I provided chaplain services for a local retirement home. The average age of residents was 82 and about 80 percent of the folks were ambulatory.

In the year and a half that I worked there, I found that contentment and happiness for older people depended a great deal on how they viewed their past. If they could say 'I did the best I could with what I had to work with,' they could be satisfied and content with their life.

On the other hand, if they were critical of themselves, felt guilt or shame about past events, or hadn't resolved events in their lives, it was more difficult for them to feel at ease with their life. It seemed to me that their contentment with their life was in direct proportion to their acceptance of how they had lived it up to that point.

One very sad case of how this worked in reverse was a couple I'll call Gert and Emory. They were in their eighties and had been together for over 60 years. Gert was very critical of her husband, and when Emory talked about their life together, he criticized decisions Gert had made, some of them dating back to the early years of their marriage. Every day, the criticism started over the breakfast table, with each one listing the mistakes the other had made.

Apparently, Gert believed that Emory was responsible for everything that did not go well in their lives. Emory gave back as mean a list of critiques as he got. Whether it was business, family relations or friends, by the time they were done with breakfast they were only halfway up to date. They finished that at lunch, with a grand finale of criticizing the decisions to move to this particular residence, even though they were living in what I would call a posh retirement facility in what was once a high-end hotel. Exhausted, they rested apart through the afternoon and ate dinner in silence. The next day they started the process all over again.

They were the most miserable people I've ever met. No one would sit at the same table with them for meals.

Gert and Emory were recounting what for them were losses, whether lost opportunities, income or status. Reliving the past, they were anything but present in the here and now, and certainly they were not enjoying the life they had achieved. Grieving their losses when they had happened might have empowered them to let go, forgive, or resolve those losses and release each other from the guilt. It seems like un-grieved losses built up and haunted them in their old age.

As I've said many times, I am the luckiest guy on the planet to have been with Marty for nineteen years. I have also been very fortunate to experience intense loss and grief without it being complicated with guilt, shame or regrets. Certainly, I made mistakes as a husband and business partner. However, none of those rise to the level of remorse now. In the months prior to her passing, Marty and I talked about regret and decided that we had none. We released any remaining feelings that we may have had over past omissions or commissions. So, we freed ourselves from regrets. My grief has, therefore, been confined to sadness.

DEALING WITH ANGER

There was one aspect of the cancer experience Marty and I had that generated real anger. That was directed at the doctor who misdiagnosed Marty's illness. It wasn't so much that he misdiagnosed it, as much as making no connections to what her symptoms might mean. During the months she saw the doctor about various pains in her bones, shoulders, ribs and neck, the doctor made no causal finding about what was happening or referral to the specialists who might have insight into what was going on. It certainly was not arthritis. The pains, it turned out, were from cancer metastasizing in her bones. Marty felt that he took choices away from her. Those choices might have been a variety of treatments or approaches, or simply a head start on dealing with the cancer.

We were both angry that this had happened. But we had to let go of those feelings so that we could focus on what we could do with the news we had and live every day as fully as possible.

MAKE HEALTHY CHOICES

My plan after Marty passed had been to stay in the home that she and I lived in since 2012 when we moved to the Gunnison Valley. It is a beautiful log home high up on the side of a mountain and has 65-mile views down the valley and mountain views all around. When our dear friend, Rachael, asked where I planned to live after Marty passed, I told her I planned to stay put. She was concerned that it would be very hard to stay there. She was right.

I tried to keep living in the house. Everything there was familiar, and a close friend lived across the road. But living in a house up on the mountain, I found that most of the time I was alone and isolated; there were no people around. The turning point came when I started working again. I would return home from a road trip to a very empty house. Even with all the wonderful memories I had of the years we had lived there, the house also held nine months of painful memories. Mostly though, it was the emptiness that got to me.

So, I made the decision to move to Gunnison, 25 miles down Valley, where I could more easily be among other people. My friend of forty years, Tam, suggested that I needed a "Marv house," a place for a soft reset and a new start. The reset was 'soft' in that I moved but stayed within my community of friends.

I was afraid that I would regret moving away from the house Marty and I had shared. My main concern was that I might be leaving behind memories or worse that I would be leaving Marty behind. Were the memories in the log walls or wood floor or the bedroom we shared? I wasn't sure.

To make certain I could take all the memories with me, I asked Carol, my therapist at the time (and co-writer now), to join me in sage smudging of the entire house. I grew up among Native Americans, had studied and practiced with Native healers and knew the power of sage and of ceremony. As we walked through the house with the sage releasing its smoke, I recalled out loud all the wonderful and painful memories in each room. We used the ceremony to lift the memories up and into my heart so they would always be with me. It worked! The memories, of course, aren't in the walls or rooms of a house. They are portable and we take them with us.

Moving was a great choice for me. It may not be for you. My advice is to make good choices for you that keep the memories intact but also give you what you need to move forward without regrets.

CHAPTER 13, COUNSELOR'S RESPONSE

In this chapter: A vast range of emotions rises up within us in our grief. As Marv showed us in this chapter, a toxic trio of doubt, regret and guilt can engulf us. We may feel they are trying to tell us something—but what? Our initial instinct is to ignore them, which is impossible; or push them away, which doesn't work for long; or minimize or bury them, which doesn't work either. They'll just resurface, and likely with a vengeance.

Importance: At various points in your life, you've probably had thoughts like these: "I knew better than to drive in bad weather." "If only I'd checked our equipment one more time." "I should have stayed with her a few minutes longer." "I should have seen this coming."

When a loved one dies, guilt (with its resulting shame) over choices we've made or regrets about our actions can develop into a judgmental condemnation of ourselves. As normal a response as guilt is, in grief, it's relentless and painful. The search for truth around the messages or thoughts that create guilt, shame, or regrets can be intense and difficult. It's vitally important to seek out companionship from others who will listen to your concerns and with whom you can share your sadness and find support. They cannot take away your pain, but they can accompany you within your experience of it.

Clinical insights: Guilt and shame are usually activated by an internal judging voice. That voice, for most of us, has existed as our judge since childhood. "One of the original functions of the judge was to act as your conscience," Byron Brown wrote in *Soul Without Shame*. "The judge learned standards of right and wrong from parents and society. Then by using guilt and shame, it helped you as a child to behave and act appropriately according to that moral code."

When we berate ourselves over a choice or a decision

concerning the death of our loved one, we're continuing to give voice to that old influence in our life—the judge. That judge always touches on something we believe is true about ourselves. We allow it to attack our self-worth as it relates to our latest alleged bad choice. Our work as adults is to disengage the judge that resides within and replace its judgments with the truth about who we are—not by superimposing another judgment, even if it's a more positive one.

"Once you know deep inside you, with a direct and felt sense, that you have inherent value and are fully acceptable to yourself, then you will begin to free yourself from the need for positive judgment and approval, from others or from your own judge," Brown wrote. "The path to truly knowing who you are requires challenging the presence of the judge. You must find the courage and wisdom . . . to see what the truth is and stay with the process of supporting that truth."

That path can lead you to be more compassionate with yourself. Brown describes the physical feeling of self-compassion as one of spaciousness in your chest, room to breathe and be with your feelings.

"The unconscious holding against the pain in the heart relaxes. You can rest in what is true: there was hurt; that can't be changed. You feel the pain, and you are larger than it. You experience a sense of allowing and support for the truth, without needing to do or be anything. The warmth of tender kindness is mixed with the cool freshness of reality."

Brown believes that "compassion is a direct antidote to the judge's poison."

Suggestions: Though we'd rather choose NOT to look at something that makes us feel bad, emotions will continue their disruption until we pay attention. Look over the following list and place a checkmark beside the feelings that stand out to you right now.

• Sadness	• Shock	• Anger	• Depression
• Despair	• Relief	• Guilt	• Bitterness
• Apathy	• Regret	• Loneliness	• Fear
• Longing	• Vulnerability	• Abandonment	• Rage
• Emptiness	• Anxiety	• Helplessness	• Detachment
• Numbness	• Emancipation	• Ambivalence	• Being Over-whelmed

Choose one of the words you checked. Focus yourself on "What does this emotion feel like?" Notice your body as you are looking for a feeling. Notice what comes into your thoughts alongside that feeling. Is a memory attached? If so, you've possibly discovered what is referred to as "unfinished business" or "an incompletion." If you've discovered something unfinished, that needs resolution. It might be best to have a trusted friend or counselor brainstorm with you about possible ways you can address it.

Identifying the feeling and recognizing any memories attached are giant steps towards discovering what's behind the emotion and what work needs to be done as a result. It allows the gift that emotions bring to us—the awareness of what is preventing us from being at peace. As you let your emotions reveal issues to you, you are the one empowered. You are taking charge of what needs doing rather than allowing power to reside in emotions.

CHAPTER 14

———

LETTING GO:
A PRIMER

Letting go is the only way to find happiness. Whatever we are attached to, Zen Master Kao Roshi taught me, we have the power to let go of. The things that draw our time, attention and energy away from being present and compassionate are the very things that keep us from being fully resilient when facing the losses life may bring our way.

Being present in the moment gives us immense power over fear, anxiety and doubt and over the thoughts, feelings, and fears that drain our resiliency. Needless to say, letting go and being present are highly interrelated and both speak to how we manage our minds.

In this chapter, I will share some of the experiences and insights I have had about letting go, which were either learned or brought into focus by the loss of Marty's life and the grief that followed. In the next chapter, I will do the same about being present.

THE WAY TO BE HAPPY

I have attachments that have caused me to lose happiness and have diminished by resiliency. The most troublesome are those I would call 'thought habits.' This is a term I've used in my consulting business to describe how organizational cultures are perpetuated, or how people within organizations settle into a way of thinking that restricts progress. On an individual level, thought habits describe how we stay as we are and are less able to adapt to changing circumstances, such as a major loss. Thought habits keep us from seeing the options and choices that are there for us.

As a young man, for example, I thought I had to be married to be happy. I was raised in a culture where that was the message. We are often not conscious about expectations that are deep within our own culture. The cultural message I inhabited left out a whole lot of other choices and ways of being happy. A notion left unquestioned, as this one was with me, can lead to poor choices, diminish our true selves and bring unhappiness to our families. Years later, as an adult with children of my own, Marty helped me get beyond that expectation. By loving me unconditionally before we talked about marriage, she helped me clearly see the choice I was making and the choices I had made previously.

There are thousands of examples of cultural notions that cause us to believe life should be lived a certain way. These become thought habits that are so embedded in us that we may not even be conscious of them. They hide behind a curtain, unseen by us, yet we act on them all the time.

Thought habits can keep us unaware of the moment we are living. We may fall into such thought habits as, "I'm pretty, so everyone should like me." Or, "I am not appreciated, so I'm justified in being angry." Or, "Most people are just out for themselves and cannot be trusted." The classic is, "I have to protect myself and even keep to myself, because no one will really understand, love or like me." The examples are abundant and in every one of us.

A thought habit about fear shows up when people say, "Well what I'm afraid of is...." Fear can become a habit. With the exception of an existential threat, anytime we act out of fear, we will either fail outright or fail to optimize our handling of a situation.

Attachments, like the one about fear, stop us from fully loving others and ourselves. The lists of negative ideas or emotions we can attach to are endless. What do you think yours are?

Systemic privilege, systemic racism and prejudice of all forms are broadly held thought habits that hurt a lot of people and keep our societies from advancing. These cultural, system-wide thought habits that treat people who are not like us as the 'other,' deny our common humanity, divide and weaken us as a species.

If we can become aware of, release and detach ourselves from thought habits, we can refocus on being more loving, compassionate and productive. We might have more time for self-reflection and to do what we love. We might find we have more energy and are better able to hold other people and their challenges in our hearts.

Even more to the point of dealing with grief, letting go of thought habits gives us a better chance of a resilient response when a loss happens.

The three letting-go ideas I want to focus on—control, past and future—are important because they can steal or diminish our resiliency.

LETTING GO OF CONTROL

Control is a myth. I can barely control myself on a good day and we don't control other people or events. But we can influence both.

As parents of young children, we have to exert a form of control—set rules and make sure our children follow them for their own safety. But when my son, Seth, turned 19, I realized that the time to 'control' him had passed. He was now an independent adult. My job had evolved, and my new parental role was to learn everything I could from him. Giving up control and a dominant position vis-a-vis my son changed everything about our relationship, and that continues today. Our age difference is 25 years. He is smarter, funnier, faster and wiser than me. We have a fabulous relationship and a part of that is due to me giving up control.

A fun instance of that relinquishing of control came during our last father-son wrestling match. He was 19 and I was 44. We had always wrestled each other, dating back to when he was a little boy. I had been a high school and college wrestler, so I had all the moves you would expect, and I had taught him some over the years. But when Seth and I wrestled on the floor of his apartment one afternoon, the tide turned. At the end of that match, I had bruised ribs, a finger pointing to the side at a very strange angle and a rug burn on my forehead. Control of my son and the wrestling match was over, finis! He was too strong and fast for me. It was an awesome moment, and we still laugh about it today. But it served as a lesson about control.

When Marty and I learned about her cancer, any control we thought we had over our future vanished. Very soon, we let go of any notion that we were going to control this disease. The only control we had left was how we were going to respond.

Choosing what to let go of and what not to let go of is wisdom. What we did NOT let go of was each other.

LETTING GO OF THE PAST
We cannot change the past, or even influence it. We *can* let go of it, so it no longer continues to harm us or prevent us from living in the present moment.

When we learned about the cancer, the past no longer mattered, and the future we thought we'd had went away. When Marty died, for a while all I felt all I had was the past and the memories. I couldn't imagine a future without her.

Zen wisdom says that when we are thinking about either the past or the future, we are not living in the present moment. True, that.

Letting go of the past should not mean letting go of precious memories or forgetting lessons we learned. It is what Dominique Boisjoli reveals to us through her paintings: Our life experiences keep adding texture, beauty, and color to whomever we become.

The experiences that we can and should let go of are those that hurt us when they happened and continue to inflict harm. We all have these encounters. We also all have the power to let go of them. Marty let go of the sexual abuse that harmed her as a young girl, so that she would not live her life as a victim. I had to let go of the anger over beatings from my older brother, so that they could no longer harm me.

The past cannot continue to hurt us unless we allow it to. A physical therapist taught me there is a difference between hurt and harm. Hurt wounds when it happens. Harm is when the injury continues to debilitate beyond the initial injury. If we allow past hurts to continue to hurt, they harm us today by stealing the resiliency we need to live now.

We can only be where our body is. If our mind is in the past, we are not present. This notion has helped me immensely. It has allowed me to be present in this moment. This has helped me let go of the past and of the future and to focus on NOW.

LETTING GO OF THE FUTURE

Planning for the future is one thing; worrying about it is quite another. Where planning for the future is wise and makes common sense, worry about the future is debilitating and delays the healing of our bodies, hearts, minds and souls.

One of the gifts Marty continues to give me is this insight: "Given the impermanence of life, every day is a gift." Knowing that I do not know if I have another day, a year or a decade to live gives me a sense of urgency and freedom to live every day to the fullest. Impermanence can look like doom, or it can look like inspiration. How we see it is a choice we make every day.

I have spent much of my life thinking about the future. But once I lost Marty, the future seemed uncertain. For many of us—and certainly for me—it seemed at first that all I had was the past.

I have learned from this grief experience that every time I find myself wondering and worrying about the future, I lose ground in moving forward. Any time I am less than present in the moment, I lose the sense of being alive. Resiliency for me depends on being aware of myself in the moment, and that makes it possible to experience the joy of being alive.

The more we can let go of the past and of the future, the easier life becomes for us. Letting go helps us get over ourselves and our sense of self-importance. We can lose sight of how the Universe, or God, or a force of nature is trying to help us. Letting go of the past and the future helps us be poignantly aware of our situation, those around us and the possibilities life presents.

Letting go of worries about the future gives us more energy, time and focus which we can direct to healing our bodies, feelings, thoughts, relationships, and loved ones. These are the things that require our attention after a profound loss of a loved one.

HOW CAN I LET GO?

Much has been said about how to let go. Some of it is religious in nature, such as forgive and forget. I can speak only for myself on this; I do not consider myself more knowledgeable than the next human. My meditation practice leads me to let the thoughts arise, label them as about the past or the future, and let them go without engaging them or attaching to them.

We can also let go by doing something that requires all of our attention. That way, we aren't thinking about anything except what we are doing. One of my favorite poems is "Buddha Shoveling Snow" by Billy Collins. Buddha and his companion do one thing for hours—scoop snow out of the driveway. Buddha doesn't talk. "He has thrown himself into shoveling snow/ as if it were the purpose of existence…." It's an awesome poetic reminder of what being present looks like.

As an adult I have gravitated to activities that require all of my attention, the kind that force me to be completely present. Scuba diving, mountain climbing and car racing, for instance, all have consequences if I were to lose focus. Fishing, hunting and photography also require my full attention and force me to be completely in the moment. During the time I'm engaged and fully present, I'm letting go of the future and the past. It is great training and confirmation that I can do this.

What are your activities that demand all of your attention? Engage them. They'll help you practice letting go. You can do this!

How to let go of control of the past and the future begins, I believe, with a decision that has two parts. One is, I want to change, meaning I want to let go of some of the past and the future and be more present. The other is, I can change myself if I want to.

We have to change the way we think in order to let go. It's a struggle, but if we don't have the power to change ourselves, we have no power at all. We can only influence others, events and the future by being willing to change ourselves and the way we think. I know this from my change management business. I've seen that the dirty little secret is that nothing will change unless you change yourself.

A practical way to let go of the past or the future, or control for that matter, is to substitute those thoughts with acceptance of yourself and your life. Sometimes, particularly after a loss, it isn't easy to see how fortunate we are to have experienced the love and life we had with our loved ones who have passed. This isn't Pollyanna. When the darker thoughts about the past or the future come to mind, we can put them aside and instead accept ourselves and our life as it is. This has been a significant way for me to let go of the pain of losing Marty—thinking and saying that I'm the luckiest guy I know.

So, let's make decisions to let go of control of the past and the future. Let's make the decision to grab hold of the power to change ourselves.

We will talk about the remarkable rewards of being present in the next chapter.

CHAPTER 14, COUNSELOR'S RESPONSE

In this chapter: When I first saw Marv's words "letting go," I found myself in a visceral struggle with emotions. Perhaps you had a similar reaction. I had suffered a recent loss and, depending on where you are in your grief experience, you're either considering what "letting go" could mean or you balked, as I initially did, and thought, "I don't want to, I'm not ready. I'm afraid I'll forget special things about my loved one if I let go." But let's talk about what 'letting go' is really about.

Importance: "Letting go" is NOT a suggestion to allow cherished memories or your deep affection for your loved one to slip away. Neither is it a hope that all the sadness and pain around your loss will simply sail off into space and be gone. The reference is to the parts of your sadness that keep you in deep suffering, such as a fear of living alone, anxiety about the future and guilt over things done or not done. Those are parts of grief that can continue to haunt and hurt you, that need to be recognized and hopefully released.

Clinical insights: In order to let go of something, you need to identify it. There may be, for instance, regret around the death of a loved one. One example might be about not getting a second opinion when an illness set in. "The emotion of regret can be all-consuming and destructive," Windy Dryden, a cognitive behavior therapist noted in an article in *The Guardian*, adding,

> "It is exhausting, it sucks all joy and fulfillment from our days and leaves us stuck, always looking backwards and unable to move forward in our lives. . . . When we are trapped in this cycle of regret, characterized by rigidity and inflexibility, we only seem able to blame ourselves for what has happened, rather than seeing our behavior in a wider context and understanding why we took the path we did based on the information we had at the time. Under these conditions, regret will become toxic."

The first step is to understand the source of the regret and how the decision to act or not was made, which adds historical sense and context to understand how it happened. With this added meaning, the regret becomes more understandable, and we can change our entire view of it. In other words, we get things wrong sometimes.

"We need permission to make mistakes, regret them, and then learn from them," Dryden noted. "There is a tendency to see the pathway you didn't take as inevitably better than the pathway you did. It may well be that this other pathway would have worked out better—but the point is we cannot know for sure. ... It can only ever be a supposition, that is the hallmark of toxic regret. "

Suggestions: Knowledge like this allows us to understand choices we made and choose to "let go" of taking responsibility for things out of our control. If you were actually responsible for some level of harm, then do what you can to repair damage that may have been done. Regrets can be an opportunity to do things differently another time. At the root of your discontent, notice if the feelings are of sadness, loss and disappointment—those feelings are a healthy part of your grieving life.

Notice what it is that hurts you. Letting go of unhealthy beliefs you may be holding might be a way of turning the tide on some of the pain inside your loss.

Here are some actions you can take to help release regrets or feelings of guilt:

1. Ask what the regret is. How did it come about? For instance, were you selfish or neglectful?
2. Write it down. Tell a counselor or trusted friend. Get it out of its secret hiding place—out of your internal dialogue. Revealing the secret is part of the battle.
3. Rather than view regret as a threat, see it as an alert that something within you needs tending.
4. Ask yourself: If you could do it over, what different action would you take? Would it have made a difference?

5. Grieve the choice you made. Understand you made your choice based on the knowledge available to you and you were doing your best with what you had.
6. Choose to forgive yourself. Let the regret go by any ritual action you choose. You can burn a scrap of paper on which you've written the regret, throw a rock into a river as a sign you are letting go or light a candle.
7. Remind yourself whenever you remember the regret that you've forgiven yourself.

.

CHAPTER 15

STAYING PRESENT
IN THE MOMENT

"Holding" each other is an important part of being present in the moment with each other. This is what my meditation guide, Andrea Balboni, refers to as the ability to 'hold' another person in your heart. That is, to keep the person safe within our hearts with acceptance and love and without judgment. This we can do even when our loved one is working through fear, anxiety, anger and other strong emotions. Though we did not have this language at the time, Marty and I were able to 'hold' each other in this way. It allowed us to be still and quiet our thoughts while we mentally and emotionally embraced each other. This would happen whether we were sitting silently beside each other on the front step or listening while the other was talking. Holding each other inside our hearts essentially brings the other person inside us where we accept and love them unconditionally.

Being present meant I could listen to Marty as she slept and know when she needed pain medication. It meant I could share how I was feeling when I needed to, and she could listen. When I was present, I could really listen, not just to the words but also to the daily thoughts Marty had or hear her deepest feelings when she shared them in the middle of the night or after the latest diagnosis. That is the key. When we are present, we can be there with and for each other. We cannot be fully present if we are distracted by our own thoughts about either the past or the future.

CRITICAL DECISIONS

Aline, a health care and hospice professional, was there to help me through difficult decisions, particularly at the end of Marty's life. When Marty was no longer fully conscious, the question was whether to stop giving her intravenous fluids. To continue the fluids was simply to keep her body functioning. That was not at all what she wanted. Still, for me, it was a very, very hard moment. Aline helped me understand the situation and the choice in front of me. I could not allow myself to be numbed by the pain and fear that was coursing through me. I had to be fully present, fully aware of Marty, of myself, and what I had to do. Though I can still recall the sadness I felt in that moment, I have no regrets over the decision. 'No regrets' appears to be, for me at least, another benefit of being able to be fully present when hard decisions have to be made.

During her illness, Marty was fully present—mentally, emotionally and physically. That allowed both of us to experience together the hard parts, the funny parts, the sadness, the fear, the loss and the love. When I was overcome by fear or sadness, I shared those feelings with Marty. Because she was so fully present in the moment, she could hear, hold and embrace what I was feeling.

HOPE AND ACCEPTANCE

In meditation, I would ask for things: Give us the ability to stay present with each other through these terrible events. Keep our love strong. Help our children deal with this. Help Marty deal with the impacts of her treatments. Give us the wisdom to know what we need to know when we need it. Give me the cancer, I'll take it. Give me strength, just give me strength. These are the things I had hoped for when all of this was happening.

In the midst of a life-taking disease, I found myself less and less focused on hope and more on getting through the day or the night. The future seemed to go away the day we got the call about her cancer. Every time we hoped for a better diagnosis, hopes were dashed. So, I stopped hoping for a different outcome. So had Marty. That was helpful. Putting a lot of effort into hope took energy away from being fully present with the reality of our situation. No doubt hope is a powerful force to help people cope in many situations. For us, though, we came to a place of peace when we accepted the diagnosis without hoping for a different fate.

When faced with a tough diagnosis or the death of a loved one, we all deal with the balance between hope and acceptance. Your journey may have already taken you to that intersection. We make our decisions at the time we need to make them. After we learned that Marty did not have the genetic markers to make her a candidate for immunotherapies, I let go of hope. That was the moment for me. I cried in Dr. Patel's office as Marty held my hand. It was time to move into full acceptance that Marty was going to die. As hard as that moment was, it was freeing as well. I could be even more fully present with her. Acceptance is a vital force that helps us stay present.

THE AFTERWARDS

After Marty passed away, I had to work hard—very hard—to stay present. I walked several times a day to let my brain use both sides. I meditated multiple times each day to try to be fully present in my body. I slept a lot. Sleep gave my brain and my aching body time to rest and restore themselves. In meditation, I was trained to focus on my breathing. That helped more than anything. As long as I was breathing, I knew I was alive. I could focus on my breath and be present in my body. I worked continuously to slow my breathing, which I knew would lower the stress in my body and, in turn, in my mind. This is not magic. We are built this way. Slowing my breathing, slowing my mind made it possible for me to stay present in the moment.

In my grief, my mind was wandering all over the place. Whether I was driving, eating, walking, cleaning the house, talking on the phone—you name it—I had a hard time staying present in whatever I was doing. I had to work hard to focus on the thing I was doing and only that thing. Thinking only of what you are doing is essentially being present. Have you ever been driving and realized you don't recall getting to where you are? In a conversation, it means you are really listening and responding to what the other person is saying, rather than, while they are talking, you are thinking what you are going to say next.

CONVERSATIONS

For 19 years Marty and I mind-shared everything—kids and family, business and work, money, philosophy, politics. We talked through every decision together. We sorted out and solved problems together. We traveled together for business and when we were not on the road with clients, we worked together in our home offices developing the business in all of its many facets. We held nothing back from each other. That was our bond: to be emotionally accessible to each other, no matter what.

For a good while after Marty died, I felt the profound loss of not being able to talk with her, to hear her thoughts or share mine. The enormous mind space we shared was now a vacuum with nothing in it. Our conversation was one of the primary places where we were both fully present with each other. Now it was lost.

I asked myself, "How can I continue the conversation?" Carol, along with Tam, my friend for more than forty years, helped me with this. They suggested I simply talk with Marty and share whatever I wanted in whatever way felt okay. So, I started going to the cemetery, sitting with my back up against one of the old Cottonwood trees and chatting with Marty about what was happening or what was on my mind and heart. It gave me immediate relief. I somehow knew that she would be listening.

While I'm careful about how I describe this, at times it has felt like a two-way communication. I have asked her, 'Are you happy?' I heard in my own mind that she answered immediately that she is happy, and I have wished her happiness often. I asked if she knows what I'm thinking, and the immediate reply was 'Only those thoughts you want me to know.' I asked if she knows how much I love her? Answer, 'Yes.'

I have no explanation for this. I'm just present in it. What I do know is that to listen this way, I have to stop. Stop thinking, stop doing, stop everything else so I can listen and be one with it in the moment. Marty and I have always been very connected since the moment we first met, and that connection continues, though in a very different way. I see her in the beauty of sunrises and sunsets. I hear her in the call of the Mourning Dove sitting outside my window. She is not here, but we are connected.

This understanding of our continuing relationship has evolved as I've moved through the grief experience. I feel her presence in my heart, and I feel joy in knowing of her continued existence and happiness. Each of us in our own way figures out how the relationship continues.

This perspective on our relationship has helped me build resiliency. Experiencing it in the way I have has made it possible for me to keep a presence within the relationship with Marty while moving forward and reconstructing my life.

A CHILD'S PLACE

The son of a friend of mine recently lost his wife. His two children are very young. His 4-year-old son was struggling with 'Where is Mommy?' Late at night, he would ask his Mom to come to him, and the next morning he was sad and disappointed that she hadn't come. The dad and grandmother thought it might help if he had a place he could go to talk with and be with her. They created a fairy garden just outside the back door of the house and placed a child-sized chair inside the garden. Now when he wants to talk with his mommy, he sits in the special garden and talks with her. It has truly calmed his heart.

Perhaps it helps to have a 'place' to talk with our loved ones who are not here with us in the physical sense of being with us. While I experience Marty being wherever she wants, I particularly see her in nature.

ONE PLACE AT A TIME

Mountain climbing, scuba diving, car racing, or hunting demand all of my attention. Singing or playing music, painting or dancing or other activities may work for you. Anything that requires all of our attention all of the time we are doing it helps us train ourselves to be present. We can only be where our bodies are.

For a long time, I was equally fine with dying or staying alive. I found that to be a very peaceful mental place to occupy. Then about two years after Marty passed, I began to care more about living than dying. That's when I found my old anxieties coming back. Marty's death has invited me and forced me to embrace the impermanence of life. The more I become comfortable with it, the better I am at staying present. I don't think about or worry about the future as much. I know I will die. I embrace that and accept it. I'm now back to being as interested in living as I am okay with dying. This helps keep me from having too much concern about the future, and it gives me more energy for living one day at a time.

My hope for your future and mine is that we find ways, even in the midst of the pain of losing a loved one, to find moments when we can be fully present and experience the resiliency that is within us.

A TIME AND A PLACE

As I moved through the emotional waves of grief, eventually I was able to set aside a time to consciously grieve. I did it daily for a while, then began to space it out as I needed. Often, I would go to a special, beautiful place in nature or a park or the cemetery and spend time there with my thoughts, memories and feelings.

This was not possible in the early months, when the grief was still overwhelming and would rise up spontaneously, as I mentioned earlier. I cannot recall when I was able to set aside time. That's not important, because these evolutions within the grief process happened differently for each of us. Whenever it was, it happened when I began to be ready to re-establish my life. I asked Carol how I might integrate grieving into that life. She suggested I set time aside for it. It worked. When I was outside of the time and place I set aside to grieve, I could concentrate and be present to do those things which restored my resiliency. It was one of the most important steps I took to move forward with my life.

LETTING OTHERS HELP

During the nine months of Marty's illness, I was able to be with her continuously. Staying present is facilitated by managing time, but it took a team effort to help me be with Marty all the time.

At the company Marty and I ran, Jeremy Stephens had been with us for some seven years when we learned about the cancer. Jeremy and Marty were great friends. On opposite ends of the political spectrum, they would laugh and kid each other with funny political dialogues. The moment he found out about Marty's cancer, Jeremy stepped up to take over my responsibilities of leading the company. He kept up with customers and managed cash flow so that I could be at home with Marty for those months, weeks, days, hours and minutes. Four years later, Jeremy continues in that role and is a partner in the business.

After hearing about Marty's diagnosis, Kevin Brown, our friend and corporate attorney, called to tell me he would handle a difficult negotiation we were in the midst of. He made it clear he would not accept any money for doing it.

I've already written about the thoughtful home health and hospice staff members who came into our home to care for Marty. These angels gave me guidance and instructions and made it possible for me to be a husband, and not solely a full-time caregiver.

My mom, Shirley, dearly loved Marty and sent us funds periodically to help with financial stresses. Neither of us was working and Marty's care was costly.

I am a very fortunate man. Countless friends and neighbors helped us during that time. I am deeply appreciative of that. But my gratitude extends even further, for the way they gave the time that made it possible for me to focus on caring for Marty—to stay on purpose and be present.

CHAPTER 15, COUNSELOR'S RESPONSE

In this chapter: The state of "being present" that Marv describes takes time and practice to achieve. As he has found, it can bring calm to the chaos of our thoughts. Since grief is famous for creating disorientation, which is accompanied by a pronounced 'inability' to remain focused, it's important to be patient with yourself as you become familiar with what it means to truly focus. Patience is vital to any new challenge, but it is especially important when you are grieving.

Importance: One outcome of learning how to "be in the present" is the ability to find a calm mental and physical posture within which you can clear your mind. You can set yourself up for a specific time to spend processing thoughts, particularly those that continue to fill you with fear, guilt or extreme sadness. Those thoughts, with all their associated pain, rage, depression, shame and self-blame can and do interrupt normal functioning. If not acknowledged or placed into the past, they can create a sense of despair. Placing the actual details of a traumatic event, such as a death, safely into the past, even if only for a period of time, gives us a sense of control over the experience and the terror of it.

Clinical insights: A goal for spending time to think about our grief is to acknowledge and confront feelings and spend time looking at our pain—and then take a respite from the experience. This experience doesn't have to focus exclusively on difficult feelings. It can be a time to reflect on happy memories of our loved one. A good term for actually accomplishing a goal of regularly focusing on our loved one in such a way is "dosing." Dosing refers to doing this work at a certain time of day, in a certain place, for a designated period of time.

Early in grief, choosing a specific period of time to set aside for dosing may not be possible. Thoughts of a loved one already fill most waking hours. Dosing is a goal. Some people eventually look forward to a specific hour during which they focus entirely on their loved one. It's like a dose of medicine that we take at a regular time and that keeps our loved one from being forgotten. At other times of day, we can then focus on activities that must take place as we move forward with our lives.

The Dual Process model of grief, introduced by Dutch researchers Margaret Stroebe and Henk Schut, "proposes that adaptive coping is composed of confrontation-avoidance of loss and restoration stressors. It also argues the need for dosage of grieving, that is, the need to take respite from dealing with either of these stressors, as an integral part of adaptive coping." Mark Henricks, *How to Use Grief Dosing to Get Through the Day*.

The idea that love does continue beyond death is supported by the current Continuing Bonds model. "We stay connected through the stories we tell about our deceased loved ones." Klass, Dennis, and Walter, Tony, "Processes of grieving: How Bonds are Continued", in *Handbook of Bereavement Research: Consequences, Coping and Care* by Stroebe, Hansen, Stroebe & Schut.

Citing Doughty, E.A., Wissel, A., & Glorfield, C. (2011). "Current Trends in Grief Counseling", http://counselingoutfitters.com/vistas/vistas11/Article_94,—"Throughout the 20th century, one of the predominate beliefs about successful bereavement was that people needed to sever ties with the deceased in order to achieve a healthy resolution to their grief (Freud, 1917/1957; Silverman & Klass, 1996). It was believed that grief had a distinct ending point allowing the bereaved to put the past behind them and move forward with life without looking back (Rosenblatt,

1996). While there are credible arguments regarding the maladaptive nature of some attachments to the deceased (Field & Bonanno, 2001; Field, Gal-Oz, & Bonanno, 2003), numerous researchers now believe that for many people, continuing bonds with the deceased is a normal part of healthy adaptation (Klass & Walter, 2001; Klass, Silverman, & Nickman, 1996; Wortman & Silver, 2001).

Klass and Walter (2001) identified four ways in which many bereaved individuals maintain bonds with the dead. The first involves sensing the presence of the dead. The authors reported that many bereaved individuals feel that their loved one is near even years after the death. The second area of continued bonds is talking to the dead. Though the authors reported there has been little research addressing how often the bereaved talk with their lost loved ones, it appears that many people carry on conversations with the departed. A common place for such conversations is at the deceased's grave. The third type of continuing bond is the use of the deceased as a moral guide. The bereaved will often times see the deceased as a role model to which they can aspire or they may think about how the deceased would have handled particular situations they are currently facing. Additionally, the bereaved may adopt (or reject) the value system of the deceased or integrate their memory into their lives in such a way that helps to define who they are. The fourth category of continuing bonds deals with the bereaved talking about the deceased. Many who have lost a loved one will talk to others who knew the dead in the hopes of knowing more about the one they have lost. The authors gave the example of a father who talked with his late son's teenage friends to get a clearer picture of all aspects of his son's life, thus continuing the relationship."

Suggestions: What can happen during times of dosing is anything from looking at old photographs to recalling difficult interactions to ruminating on how life was and how it is now. Anything goes.

Some ideas for setting up a dosing practice:
• Set a specific place, where you won't be interrupted
• Set a certain time to begin and end (30 minutes to an hour, or whatever is repeatable regularly)
• Have paper/pencil/drawing tools handy, along with photographs, your journal, a piece of clothing or familiar item that belonged to your loved one, music your loved one enjoyed, even their favorite movie.

Some ideas for dosing activities:
• Draw something for them or sketch a memory for yourself
• Write in your journal about them
• Draw a picture of yourself as you presently are feeling
• Take a walk through your loved one's favorite area
• Go on a bike ride—if they enjoyed doing that
• Make their favorite snack

In short, do whatever allows you to focus on them and on your memories with them. Spend this time at the same time each day and put your whole self into the activity. Cry or laugh or yell—don't hold anything back. When your time is up, do something else entirely. Repeat this daily—it can go on forever if you wish.

The point is to keep connected through memories, honor your loved one and allow productive time to actively grieve their loss. You may find yourself putting random thoughts on hold in order to focus on them during the next day's dosing time. You also may begin to look forward to the special time of remembering. Do remember to end your time by shifting into activities focused on your other loved ones or interests.

CHAPTER 16

A SENSE OF PURPOSE

There are times in our lives when we may ask ourselves, what is my purpose in life: Why am I here? For nearly two decades my primary purpose was to be the best husband I could be to Marty. There is interplay between finding life's purpose and letting it find you. I feel the universe brought Marty and me together, and within that we found a single purpose to love each other well. Within the relationship, we explored our deepest thoughts, desires and feelings.

When Marty passed, I was lost. I felt as though I was being crushed under 100-foot waves of grief. I couldn't breathe. I was dying. I thought at first that I had simply lost my sense of direction. But direction is where you are headed. I was struggling with something more profound: my sense of purpose. Purpose is who you are and why you are here. It goes to the heart of the matter: Did I want to continue living, and why?

Can there be a single purpose for a life when we have multiple relationships? On one level, we can articulate our reasons for doing what we do in terms of our role in our family, our workplace or our friendships. We carry a sense of intention, for instance, when planning for our kids' education, for where we'll live or for our retirement. We do the same in our work lives, be it advancing our careers or mentoring young people.

The purpose was to be the best husband I could be, for Marty to be the best wife she could be and to love each other well— these intentions put everything else we did in perspective. The relationship was the organizing priority, around which everything else revolved. We would say, "If we are okay, then everything else is okay or will be soon." We felt we were living something larger than just ourselves. Our relationship was our "third," a unique creation of our own making. Marty's happiness was, for me, as important or more so than my own. She felt the same way. That definition of love has not changed for me. Where I can share that reservoir of love has changed and is now more about spreading it around.

My life's purpose left me the day Marty passed away. It was as simple and painful as that. Of course, I had memories and was deep in the grief process in the months following. But early on, I felt that loss of purpose. I didn't know what to do with myself. I couldn't work and didn't have the mind space to write, except in the journal I started. Close friends took me fishing, because I did not have the energy to get the boat in the water and go fishing myself. About the only thing I could do for a while was take three or four walks a day to re-ground myself on planet earth, get my body and mind working together and start healing my heart.

In my consulting business, we help governments and not-for-profits define their purpose in terms of what experiences they want to create for customers. A state or local government might want to make sure snow is cleared from roadways before the school bus schedule kicks in or prevent domestic abuse or take steps toward cleaner water. As long as a government focuses on its customers, it can be straightforward in identifying the purpose of public services. That purpose guides budget decisions, performance measurements and service delivery strategies. So, I am very keyed into the importance of identifying what the purpose is.

We create a sense of purpose for ourselves as well as for those we love and those who depend on our support, guidance, leadership, love or partnership. A person who is unclear about their purpose is not in a very good position to provide any of these things for others. Without purpose, we wander. Without purpose, we are easily taken in any direction events or others wish to take us.

When I was missing a sense of purpose, I felt diminished and confused. I didn't really know for sure why I was here, what my life was about. It wasn't enough to simply continue to breathe and take up space because I could. I needed to redefine and restore a purpose that was larger than myself, and one that would move my life forward.

In those early days of grieving, I became aware of how important it was to restore my reservoir of resiliency. Next was to answer the question: What purpose do I have in being here? If I was going to restore my resiliency and reconstruct my life, to what end would I do so? Rediscovering a sense of purpose put into perspective everything I was doing to recover. Restoring my resiliency became important so that I could live with an open heart and recover from the loss.

When I define my purpose in terms of my open heart, I am choosing to bypass what I do and the roles I play and look inward. I say that I am the condition of my heart. My purpose is to keep it open to life, to others and to love, to what the universe may teach me. I want to be grateful for this gift of being alive as a human being. I want to give more than I get. There is more reward in giving than in receiving. My dopamine hit—my deep sense of pleasure—comes when I give something of myself.

For me, engaging life with an open heart and mind applies to all aspects of life—to everything I do, say and am involved with. Marty taught me what it meant to live with an open heart and I'm doing everything I can to carry that forward in the life I have now. Many times, and on many days, I may not yet know what that means or where it will take me, but it is definitely how I want to live my life. My experience tells me that living with an open heart makes me stronger and gives me the resiliency to face whatever life brings, be it good, bad or otherwise.

Engaging life with an open heart is taking a particular stance. It is an active way to engage others and stay open to the possibilities of every relationship. As I continue to grieve the loss of Marty, I find that I can put all of my experiences in the context of engaging with an open heart. When my heart is most open, I am the most resilient. When I struggle to keep it open, I also struggle to have the resiliency I need and want. An open heart makes it possible for me to be open to the emotions that come up in the grief process. We know that facing and embracing our emotions is critical to rebuilding resiliency. Thanks to wise teachers and coaches, I have learned to hold others in my heart and to remove from my body the negatives that have settled into me from past losses and hurts.

A last word about the idea of living with the purpose of an open heart: Doing so makes me vulnerable to life, to disappointments and to losses. It allows life to tear some holes in me. But it also opens me to the wonder of people, of life and even of the possibilities to love again. I choose to be vulnerable to life and open to its possibilities.

A Reconstruction Project

I recall hearing Joe Biden tell the story of how his father took the long walk up the apartment stairs to tell his family that he had lost his job. Their family made adjustments to keep moving forward. His father found a job many miles away and came home on weekends to be with the family. They were united in their goals of staying together, staying strong as a family and making it possible for the kids to go to college. We know the results. Resiliency is indeed a way of life. The resiliency that the Biden family built into their children helped Joe when he lost his wife and daughter, and again when his son Beau died from cancer. Building resiliency into our families promotes that kind of multi-generational strength that helps us handle the losses that come our way and still move forward to reconstruct life.

I consider my life a reconstruction project. I am a project, so to speak, where the goals are to rebuild resiliency, purpose, hope, and enough happiness to make it worthwhile. Friends, family and Carol, have helped me navigate what is at times a difficult path. They have listened deeply and shared insights when things have been difficult and celebrated with me when the reconstruction takes a step forward.

IDENTIFY YOUR PRIORITIES

I was looking for a purpose in life that is larger than myself. Most of the time we think of that in terms of a profession or making a difference in the world or in terms of our families. As we move through our lives, it is easy to take purpose for granted: Life will always be there. After the death of a significant other, it may not be there; it may be lost, as it was for me. A sense of our purpose can change or shift over time as we experience the loss of a loved one, a change in physical abilities or spiritual growth.

It took about a year and a half for me to come to clarity about my newly acquired sense of purpose that undergirds my approach to life. Although it has seeped into everything I do, I still needed priorities within that purpose. Here they are:

Make a Difference: I have a strong belief and lots of proof that my business makes a difference in the lives of people who work in government and in those they serve. It continues to be important to my life and that is why I continue to work. Making a difference is a priority within the larger purpose of living with an open heart. As you might guess, volunteering with Living Journeys also falls within this priority.

Relationships: In the same way that Marty and I made our relationship our top priority, connections with people continue to be of greatest importance to me. Relationships with children, grandchildren, relatives, friends and community members are among the most complex interactions we have and the place where we discover who we are and how to be human.

Be Free: Personal freedom to live the life I want is another high priority for me. After my children's mother and I divorced, I paid child support. In those days, the courts, law enforcement and every agency within the child support system used the term "child support obligors" to describe those of us who paid child support. In other words, the system was telling those who paid child support that we did so because we were obligated to do so. I found it a confusing message for my children. I paid support because I wanted to and felt responsible to do so, never because I was obliged to do so. Many fathers I knew at the time felt the same way. Yet the culture at that time demeaned the motives of the parent who did not have custody and who paid child support. I made a decision at that time that I would never do anything because I was obligated to. Today, the only thing I do, because I am required to, is to obey laws and pay taxes. Everything else I do I want to do. With that history in mind, it is my third priority to sustain my personal freedom, to act in ways that are consistent with my values and beliefs and are respectful of others.

STAYING ON PURPOSE

Keeping an open heart is a challenge. The world might just crush it. In fact, it probably will crush it. No, it *will* crush it. There, that's more honest. But in spite of how you might get hurt, if living with an open heart is your purpose, you live with the risk, remind yourself why you are doing it and dust yourself off when misfortune happens.

Marty and I had spoken of living with an open heart many times during our years together. But during the depths of my grief, the idea was hidden behind my sadness. Over time, though, living with an open heart emerged as the reason I am here, the base for my approach to life and my purpose in living.

Priorities are about where you spend your time, your emotions, your thoughts and your resources. Defining priorities make it surprisingly easier to understand or even define purpose. So, you may discover your priorities then your purpose. It's like if an organization can decide what results it wants to achieve for customers, it is then much easier to define the mission. It just happened in the reverse order for me: purpose first, then priorities.

My purpose and my priorities are why I volunteer my time with Living Journeys, a not-for-profit in the Gunnison Valley dedicated to supporting cancer patients and their families. That work is mostly about making a difference, but it is also about building relationships with others on the cancer journey.

What those priorities are matters only to you. The process is like strategic planning: You create strategic priorities and identify the results that you want to achieve within each one. They are yours, they work for you and so you have them as a context within which to make decisions. I've shared mine here not because I think they should be anyone else's, but because they illustrate what purpose and priorities can look like and what they can do for you. Having broad priorities gives me a lot of freedom to choose what to do and how to spend my time, energy and resources within those priorities.

For me, setting priorities and knowing my purpose cuts across every aspect of life. They have been essential to moving forward and building resiliency. Having them in place has given my life direction and meaning that was missing for a good while. I encourage you to discover or rediscover your purpose and priorities. It's a good way to keep on living.

Chapter 16, Counselor's Response

In this chapter: Depending on where you are in your grief experience, defining your *purpose* is important. It can provide a focus in which to ground yourself or suggest a new direction to consider. Some days your purpose might simply be to get through the day, while other days you may be able to begin focusing on "Who am I now?" and "Why am I here?" After a death, all areas of your life are affected and exposed to change. Your role as a spouse, caregiver, or whatever you've been, is now changed. Marv was Marty's husband and caregiver. He became a single man who was no longer caregiving. That's disorienting. Changes have occurred for you but one focus you can determine that will remain is your purpose. To know your purpose provides you with a guidepost to inform daily decisions and to steer you towards an ultimate destination.

Importance: "Efforts and courage," President John F. Kennedy said, "are not enough without purpose and direction." A life's purpose is simply your life's message. It's what you wish to accomplish what drives you while you're on this Earth. In the past, you may not have felt the need to formulate a purpose statement. Now, if you find yourself floundering as you look to the future and feel little or no excitement for what lies ahead, then the exercise of identifying a purpose may be beneficial.

Clinical insights: There are many formulas for figuring out your life's purpose. Some of them are quite complicated. The simplest one I've seen is from Miriam Neff's *From One Widow to Another*:

"Consider the following:
1. What tasks have I done that brought great satisfaction?
2. What tasks do I look forward to doing?
3. What personal values are important enough to me to motivate me to act when there is no apparent reward or positive feedback for my action?
4. What activities in my life give me that feeling of anticipation, energy, and 'I can't wait to get to it?'"

Complete these statements:
1. I am energized when I'm looking forward to:
2. I would like to be remembered as a person who:
3. Past accomplishments that I treasure include:

Take the time to settle into your easy chair with a notebook and this assignment, and make these lists. Then let the lists settle for a day or two. What else comes to mind? What answers seem not so important as they did at that moment? Next, talk to a few friends who know you well. . . .Do they see a match in your lists and the person they know? The final mission statement is yours alone to create, but others can provide insights and ideas."

Suggestions: In "How to Find Your Life Purpose" (https:// personalexcellence.com), Celestine Chua suggests a 30-minute writing exercise in which you record every answer your brain produces in response to "What is my life purpose?" You continue writing until "tears come to your eyes." It can take several attempts, but it is worth a try and it's interesting to see what happens.

Any of these exercises is difficult, probably impossible in early grief, but as your energy increases it may help to reassess your interests and direction. As you make a simple purpose statement (i.e., "to live to my highest potential and help relieve world hunger," or "to be my best and touch other people's hearts") it is possible that your future decisions will be more easily made and align with your interests.

CHAPTER 17

PLAYBOOK FOR HEALING

The memorial service we held for Marty and the way in which it built community was so important to rebuilding resiliency into my life and helping me heal.

A memorial service can be anything you want it to be, of course. Every religion, culture and belief system has traditions, rituals and practices around death and dying. If your family lives in New Orleans, you might hold a send-off parade led by a happy blues band. If you're Native American, you might have your loved one's body rest on a scaffold so that their spirit can depart to the next stage of their spiritual journey. If you're a practicing Hindu family living in Kathmandu, the body of your loved one would be cremated on a stack of logs and the ashes would be released into the Bagmati River so that the atman, or spirit, may transition to the next life. All cultures and traditions are intended to help us say goodbye and to heal those left behind.

I encourage you to engage in whatever practices and system of beliefs are important and meaningful to you. Mine happens to be Buddhist. Whatever it is, your belief system will help you in the healing process and hopefully contribute to the resiliency that will enable you to face life again.

MARTY' SERVICE

Two days before Marty's service, my son Seth arrived. For me, that is like sending in the Marines. He is my rock and rudder. We can talk about anything, and we know each other completely. When we hugged at the airport, we wiped back the tears and he about squeezed all the air out of me. He and Marty were very close, so he was experiencing his own grief in addition to feeling mine.

Who wants to plan a memorial service for your beloved spouse? Well, no one. But I had to, and, in the end, I wanted to. In my mid-twenties, as a young seminarian and then a local United Methodist minister, I had officiated at more than 130 funerals and memorial services. A minister, imam, priest, rabbi or any other spiritual leader can play a healing, guiding or inspirational role at transitional moments in people's lives. As a minister, I found that I could be most helpful to people who were going through the end of life and the grief processes. I owe a debt of gratitude to all of those families whom I met in their time of loss. Years later, what I learned from them informed and helped me in my own grieving process.

Relationships with the friends and relatives who came for Marty's service were and are the fabric of the life Marty and I had built together. They came out of respect and love for Marty. They also came to support me and my family and to grieve their own loss of Marty from their lives. Some were neighbors who lived just up the road in our Valley or in other small towns in Colorado; others came from Arizona and Texas. One close friend, a hunting and fishing buddy, came in from Florida to be there that day. I will never forget those who came.

The morning of the service, I woke up wondering how I would possibly get through the day. I missed Marty so much. In the quiet of my mind, I kept asking, how is it possible that she is gone? When I got out of bed that morning and walked into the bathroom, I looked to my right into her closet and saw all of her clothes hanging there waiting for her to come in and start the day. I walked in, ran my hands along her blouses, her suits, her scarves and her coats. I could still smell her sweet scent on her silk dresses. How is it possible that she is not here? This party is for her. She should be here to enjoy it. My sense of reality was confused that morning, swinging back and forth between the past and the present.

I can remember dressing that morning and finding that I could not tuck my shirt in. I always wear my shirts tucked in, yet I felt it would strangle me if I tucked in my shirt. I asked my children and a close family friend if it would look okay if I left my shirt untucked. When you are in the moment when the reality of your loss is completely real, something like tucking in your shirt might be impossible. Marty's close friend Raechel assured me it was okay.

The service we had for Marty became a powerful healing experience for my family, friends, our community and me. For that reason, I want to share the story with you. I hope you will find it illustrative of things to keep in mind.

If you have lost a loved one, you don't have to go through this alone. Seth, Nici (the hospice social worker who had been so helpful near the end of Marty's life)) and Bre (the home health caregiver who had taken such gentle care of Marty) helped plan the service. I asked Nici to officiate and Seth to read what I had written because I couldn't. Bre, who is an organizing genius, offered to plan the food, the tables, wind chimes and the pictures.

When you face the passing of a loved one, I encourage you to do two things. One, be clear about the wishes of your loved one and make sure those wishes are carried out. Second, figure out how to carry out those wishes in ways that are healing to you and others who mourn the loss.

I wanted the service to be a time to remember Marty, who she was to all of us, the impact she had on us, and what she meant to us. I wanted it to be an opportunity for us all to begin the process of healing from the incredible sadness and pain from losing her. We designed the service around the people who were experiencing the loss.

I also wanted the service to be a way to knit together the people from various parts of our lives. I wanted my son Seth and my friends living in the Gunnison Valley to know each other. Then when we talked and referenced each other, we would all understand who we were talking about. I wanted Emily and Chris, the children Marty brought to our marriage and whom I helped raise, to meet the friends Marty and I had made. I wanted Carol, our grief therapist, to know who I was talking about when I referenced the name of a relative or a friend and for friends and relatives to know who Carol was when I spoke of her. Knitting the parts of my life together was an important part of my healing. I wanted my friends and family to be one community.

So Nici, Seth, Bre and I planned the service around these ideas. First, we gave the people closest to Marty an opportunity to share their memories and love for Marty. When our son Chris got up to speak, he was almost overwhelmed by his emotions, but he dug deep and was able to share with everyone his love and thoughts of his Mom. The same for Marty's sister, Suzy, who spoke of her love for her younger sister. When close friends stood and spoke, they shared their memories and the impact Marty had on their families and their lives. Raechel, who was like a sister to Marty, spoke from her heart when she said the love she has for Marty will last for this lifetime and beyond. Kevin, our friend and our business's lawyer, moved us with his loving humor. Three weeks prior, he had come up from Austin, Texas, for a visit with the express goal of making us laugh. Andy and Stormy and Kurt shared their gratitude, love, and respect for Marty. For those who spoke it was an opportunity to express their love and their loss. Their words, their feelings, their memories were so sweet, so touching, the tears of gratitude flowed onto my cheeks.

Seth pulled from his deep internal reservoir of strength to read the statement I had written. I wanted my community to understand who Marty was in this life, the purpose with which she lived and the courage with which she died. I'm sharing it with you here and now because it was healing for me to write it and consoling for Seth to read it. People said that it was a comfort for them to hear it. I hope it is helpful to those of you who have lost a loved one.

MARV'S EULOGY FOR MARTY

These are the things Marty lived by: Be happy, live happy. It's a decision. Make the decision to be happy.

Let go of the past, just let go. It's gone, don't hang on to it or keep thinking about it. Otherwise, you can't be present in the present. Plus, it will make you unhappy if you can't let go.

Love, don't judge others on how they choose to live. We are in no position to judge anyone. Plus, it's not our job.

Lastly, and this is on Marty's card: Face death at any moment, but live life fully at all times.

She was good with Jesus—he taught us to love each other.

She was good with Buddha—he taught us how to live, how

to let go, find peace and be happy. I've always said she was born out of the belly of Buddha because she just didn't attach or spend time on things negative. She let go of the past easily and quickly. She ignored negativity, ignored negative people and when she couldn't ignore them, she just forgave them.

Marty's ultimate Zen move was to let go of this life to begin another. And she got rid of cancer on Independence Day.

Marty made a difference in the lives of people and organizations we worked with. The governments she worked with are more focused on making a difference for their customers. Many of our government customers have told us about the differences that have been made in their communities because of the work Marty did. Marty and I have been partners in all aspects of life and work.

Cancer tried but could not dampen Marty's spirit. Her smile and spirit were irrepressible. In the face of daunting odds and immense pain, she never complained, not once.

What is important for my Dad is that the bond between his heart and Marty's is unbreakable. The bond Marty and my Dad have will live on forever. She died in Dad's arms at home, right where she wanted to be.

Dad and Marty are Buddhists, as most of you know. They don't really have a belief system when it comes to the afterlife. They don't know what it may be like but are not afraid of death. There is no reason to fear the unknown.

At the end of Marty's life here, when she could not speak, she would sometimes look beyond those in the room, seeing we did not know what. Dad asked her if there is something beyond this life, Marty looked him directly in the eye, raised her eyebrows, open her eyes wide, smiled and nodded 'Yes.' So, there you have it!

From Dad and Marty's wedding vows:

I promise to live with you with an open heart, to love you, honor you and respect you from the most loving part of myself, to give you my best self, my most courageous self, my most worthy self, in the best of times and in the most difficult of times, from this point forward.

I give you my whole heart, and in this promise, I commit to giving you a heart that is joyful, adventurous and happy in life. In this promise, I also commit to turning away from fearfulness and selfishness, lest my heart become hardened or closed to you, your love and the promise of the world.

I promise to live with you in life with passion, to dream our dreams in the best of times and in the most difficult of times.

Marty to Marv—I honor your adventuresome spirit and will support your efforts to explore the deepest sea and climb the highest mountains of this world which we find so beautiful.

Marv to Marty—I honor and support your deep desire to build a home so that we may refresh our minds, our spirits and our hearts, and I commit to creating a place with you where our children, our families and our friends are always welcome.

SCARVES IN THE WIND

Marty loved scarves; I mean she LOVED scarves. And I loved buying them for her. If I was in Washington D.C., for example, I would go to the Phillips Collection or the National Gallery shops and look for scarves. Bre's brilliant idea was to hang Marty's scarves on the trees in the park surrounding the pavilion and invite everyone to take one for themselves. It was magical. During the service, they waved to us in the wind. Everyone who wanted one could take something of Marty home with them. Since then, I have seen Marty's scarves around town on friends who came to the service. Several people have mentioned to me that they wear her scarf and that it means so much to them to have something of hers. This was about doing something for someone else.

Music can heal and inspire, lift up and become salve on the soul. We chose three songs to play via a wireless speaker. "Stairway to Heaven" by Led Zeppelin "Somewhere Over the Rainbow" sung by IZ (Israel "IZ" Kamakawiwo'ole) and "Tears in Heaven" by Eric Clapton. You get the vibe. We were taking care of our hearts through the music, and we all felt lifted up by the music played at different times during the service.

The setting for the services was an outdoor park next to the Gunnison River. As I mentioned earlier, Marty's ashes and mine will go into the Gunnison River, so the setting was particularly important. There was a pavilion there, which Bre dressed up with wind chimes and ribbons. Chris, Emily, Seth, Carol and I sat at the front table where we held onto each other throughout the service. We were outside where we could all breathe and feel the warmth of the sun. I told the kids that we would always be able to see their Mom in the Colorado River system and the beauty of nature, which is where we were that day.

At the back of the pavilion, we had a table set up with an enlarged picture of Marty and family; friends had been invited to bring and share pictures of her, as well. The table was covered with photos, and it gave folks a chance to smile and say, "Remember when we did that?" Everyone was welcome to remember, to cry if they wanted and to laugh, too. Laughter is a good thing when there has been a great loss.

When the service was over, Nici invited everyone to hang out for a while, share a meal and spend time with each other before we—and anyone who wanted to join us—headed for the cemetery. We hung out around the pavilion for another hour and a half, hugging, talking, eating the great food Bre had arranged. Some who came were getting to know each other for the first time. If this had been the Sixties, we would have declared it a 'love in.' I cried quietly throughout much of the service. The hugs that followed, the conversations with dear friends and the deeply meaningful words shared continue to be healing memories for me.

The kids, me, everyone felt both sad to lose Marty and, at the same time, happy we had each other. We immersed ourselves in community and family. None of us felt alone, because we had each other. Those connections we made between people continue today. That day Marty helped us to continue to build community and strengthen family—two things she loved to do.

At the cemetery, a smaller group gathered to pay respects to Marty and continue the celebration of her life. As the afternoon sun warmed our faces, the love that we all felt for Marty and each other warmed our hearts. We stood in a circle around the gravesite, each of us having our own thoughts and feelings in those moments, and also looking into the faces of those gathered, silently exchanging compassion for each other.

I had chosen to use Marty's favorite Pueblo Indian pot as the urn for her ashes. It was a black pot from Santo Domingo Pueblo covered with squares of turquoise and sealed on top with a seed pot from Acoma, Marty's favorite Pueblos. At the cemetery, before placing the urn in the grave, I carried it around the circle so people could touch it and say what they wanted to say to Marty. Most told her goodbye and that they loved her. We need sometimes to be able to say 'goodbye' in a direct way.

Oh, one more thing. We popped champagne and toasted Marty's life. Celebration heals, too.

My friends, my hope is that the story of Marty's service is helpful to you as you consider end-of-life services and ceremonies.

Of course, there is no template for the best approach to this, as it depends on your culture, beliefs, practices and personal needs. My best wishes for you as you plan your ceremony. Reflect on all of the wonder of the life you have shared and rebuild the resiliency within you to go forward again with life.

I wrote this poem in 2019 after an experience in the Dallas-Ft Worth airport:

Scarves

She had so many
Beautiful ones
Small
Long
Lacy, Crepey

Rothko Blue
Yellow
Orange, Taupe
Melon
Delicious colors

From Branches
They Waved
Goodbye
In the Whispering
Wind

Two Years Since
She Freed Herself,
Two years that

She's been gone
Gone

Traveling thru an
Airport
There They Were
Beautiful Scarves
In a Store Window

It was Instinctive
My leaping
Heart
Wanted
To get her one

Oh my...
But She's Not Here...
Startled
Pause
What Just Happened?

The urge
To Give Her
Her next Scarf
Very Much
Alive

Almost Two Years
Now...
Loving her
As Much as Ever

How do I
Let go a Little More
And
Still Love Her
With All My Heart?

Bring Home
One Last
Beautiful
Colorful
Scarf

DOING TWO THINGS AT ONCE

Celebrating and grieving at the same time—doing two things
at once—is how I experienced the service for Marty. I'm not
inclined to gloss over anything. I believe in facing head on whatever life brings. Carol knew how much and how well Marty and
I loved each other, and she could appreciate what I meant when I
say that I'm the luckiest guy I know. As you know by now, most
of my grief has been manifest in sadness and loss, and sometimes
in celebration. That is probably a reflection of the way I face loss
and love in life as one experience.

Likewise, I am moving forward and grieving at the same
time. There is a real difference between saying I'm moving forward and saying that I'm moving on. This is an important distinc-
tion. Moving on implies I'm leaving my past behind, even leaving
Marty and our life behind. Moving on implies that I'm leaving
my grief behind as well. Neither of those things is accurate or
true. I am moving forward with this life. Marty is with me always.
I am not leaving my grief behind, either. Instead, I am accepting
grief, in its ever- changing forms, as part of my life.

Some people in grief don't want to talk about their loved one, for fear that they won't be able to move forward and build a new life. That will not facilitate the grieving process and restore resiliency. For some trying to find new loves, if it was their spouse who died, they don't feel they should or can talk about their past life and the loved one who passed away. If that is the case, you are with the wrong new lover. We can and need to be with people who accept us for who we are, that grief, loss and our loved one will always be part of us.

Two other things I do at the same time are to feel sad and happy. Honestly, before this experience, I would have wondered if that was possible or even reasonable. It's like that place in the grief process when you are tearing up and smiling at the same time. I've experienced this. I might be having sad feelings that cause me to cry but remembering wonderful moments that make me feel happy. Many feel sad and angry at the same time, or sad and guilty. You get the picture. I am guessing you have experienced two emotions at once, yourself.

We are able to grieve and move forward at the same time. We can find love again while we continue to experience the loss and honor our loved one who has passed. We can live life, embrace our losses and grow stronger in our resiliency at the same time. That's pretty incredible.

PROSPECT IN THE PARK

Recently, I visited River Park, where we had the service for Marty. I have done so numerous times, and the landscape is always as it was before the service. The pavilion is just the pavilion. The picnic-style tables are under the pavilion, as before. Benches sit beside the Gunnison River as it flows without interruption. The fresh air sweeps through the trees, as it had the day it held the scarves. The wind chimes, special table for memory photos, table mementos, the food, the people, the music, none are there now, of course.

This perspective on the Park helped me remember that the commonplace can be sacred and the sacred can be in the commonplace. This prospect is especially dear to me. It was a reminder that everything is connected with everything else. Marty and I are still connected. I hope this resembles in some way your experience of staying connected with your loved one.

CHAPTER 17, COUNSELOR'S RESPONSE

In this chapter: The word healing implies becoming whole again, recovering, returning to a condition that existed before. But we know things don't return to a condition that existed before. Our loved one is not coming back. We've seen Marv as he struggles with that reality: There is no recovery of our loved one or of 'us' as we were. Our healing must focus on becoming changed, on something we'll call integration.

Importance: There's a story in *It's Ok That You're Not Ok* by Megan Devine where she relates the experience of a man whose life's work was to restore land after it had been devastated by mining operations. Though landscapes had been destroyed and were polluted, this man worked with native tribes and researchers, who understood the geological challenges and found a way to restore the sites. The work was intensive and backbreaking. It took decades to see the results: flourishing ecosystems, along with the return of native plants and animal species.

"The earth does heal—and so does the heart," Devine tells

MARV WEIDNER & CAROL GOLDFAINDAVIS

us. "And if you know how to look, you can always see the ravages underneath new growth. The effort and hard work and struggle to make something entirely new—integrated and including the devastated landscape that came before—is always visible."

In other words, the devastation of your loss will always exist, but we are made of love and scars, of healing and grace. We can hold our scars and joy simultaneously. Recovery is what we're really looking for here, and it becomes all about listening to your wounds and cultivating patience.

Clinical observations: There is no moving ON. There is only moving WITH and integration of all that has come before, and all you have been asked to live. That is the deal—you must focus on showing patience and compassion towards yourself in order to allow the integration of the pain alongside the joy of memories of your loved one.

There is an ongoing adaptation to holding the bitter with the sweet in a unique balance that is yours alone. What you have control over is how you care for yourself within this process. The pain you feel now is connected to love. With patience, your love won't fade but the pain will. "Recovery in grief is a process of moving WITH what was, what might have been, and what still remains."—Megan Devine, *It's OK That You're Not Ok.*

Suggestions: Ultimately, we want the pain, the discomfort to stop. We want our loved one back! We know we have no ability to change what's happened, but we can choose to take baby steps towards focusing on caring for ourselves to bring forth some balance. Caring for our own heart and mind may seem oddly selfish, but it's important to give our bodies permission to stabilize.

Take a deep breath and pay attention to the simple things

that bring comfort and calm to your soul. Focus on doing those things. That is where healing lies. Eat, sleep, exercise, spend time with others, enjoy nature and reach out to help someone else.

CHAPTER 18

THE MAGIC OF EXPRESSION

At the time of Marty's passing, thoughts and feelings rushed through me so quickly I felt as though my head was literally spinning. I couldn't keep up with my own thoughts. To slow the whirlwind, Carol suggested I start a journal.

When I first began to write, I saw my thoughts as falling into one of three categories: Questions, Experiences, or Thoughts. A Question, for instance, might be, "When or will I ever be able to feel emotionally myself again?" An Experience might be, "When I'm at the cemetery I feel close to Marty." A Thought might be, "I am making the decision to be happy." I write down the Question, Experience or Thought and then I think or feel my way through to a response. That's when it gets interesting, and the growth begins.

Everyone can take his or her own approach, of course. There are excellent resources and people to guide your journaling efforts. This happens to be what works well for me. The questions, it turns out, have prompted the most interesting insights.

Responding to my thoughts, feelings and questions remains

essential to my healing process. Writing is an integrative activity that is both action and expression. Among all of my efforts to rebuild resiliency within myself, writing has been among the most productive and powerful. It continues to fuel my energy and engagement with life and provides a way to reflect on and share my experience.

Writing makes it possible for me to get it all out and be completely honest with myself, whether anyone else hears it or not. While I'm writing, my focus is strong: I am only doing that one thing. Once my thoughts are on paper, I can return to what I wrote, see what has changed and how I have evolved. I found it a great companion to the counseling Carol provided. I could bring my questions, thoughts and feelings right into the discussion with her. Even now, my journaling is helpful in sorting out my life, my questions, challenges and feelings. This is where I write poetry. As may be obvious, I am able to write this book in part because of my journaling.

Words have always been an important expression for me. When I was four years old, my great aunt called me her "talking box." As my friend Tam says, "For us, words are events."

For me, writing has been therapeutic, healing, challenging and cathartic. I would encourage you to write what is on your heart and in your mind. Some of it may surprise you, inspire you, help you grieve, understand your loss, and see how your own thoughts can move you forward.

DRAWING ON ART

Sometimes the emotions or experiences in the grief process are just too raw or too complex to be captured by words alone. I found that to be true immediately after Marty passed. As a way to release the sadness from my body, Carol thought I should draw pictures of some of the experiences. At one point, she was quite specific. She suggested I sketch a picture of Marty and me fighting the cancer together. I did, and now I have a form of expression I can go back to whenever I need it. Let me be clear: I have few to no artistic skills, but that didn't matter and still doesn't.

The image in my mind was Marty and me standing back to back, kicking and hitting cancer so hard that we knocked it backward. We fought cancer for as long as we could. It gives me strength to see us together, fighting the disease that took Marty's life. Cancer could not destroy her spirit or our love. Even today, I gain strength and I smile when I see my drawing and remember how well and how hard we fought for life.

Love cannot defeat Death

True…But

Death cannot defeat Love

So here we are in my sketch, fighting cancer back to back.

In another drawing, I depicted the moment when Marty let go, gained her independence from the cancer and passed on to what was next for her. This is perhaps the most poignant moment in our life together.

As I mentioned in an earlier chapter, when I knew she was making her transition, I lay down on the bed with her, took off my shirt so we were skin to skin and held her in the way she loved with her arms folded in front of her and her hands cupped under her chin. She had always felt secure in my arms, and I wanted her to feel that way, especially in those moments. I kissed her, told her I loved her and told her she could go on her journey without any hesitation or concern about us here. She breathed her last breath in my arms. She left, I believe, without any reservations and with a courage I can only hope all of us have in that moment. My little drawing helps me remember every moment of our final experience together.

In the weeks after Marty passed, I was trying to find a way to continue my conversations with her. Carol suggested that I draw a picture of a place where Marty and I could be together. I envisioned a high mountain ranch where Marty and I could hold hands, walk, talk and enjoy nature. Marty had a number of night dreams throughout her life where she was flying, so I drew her flying above it all. Her dogs and cats and car are there, the house we lived in and the trees outside our door. I also drew a pond with fish, birds nearby and even an elk or two. Sometimes I go there in my mind and imagine being with her for a time.

Writing about your experiences and using art are two excellent ways to express yourself and remember.

OTHER ARTS AND ACTIVITIES

Exercise is obviously good for everyone. I stopped running when I was 65 years old, and I miss it. But walking engages both sides of the brain and it is a regular part of my days. I was reminded that Darwin walked to clear his thinking. Must have worked! Exercise has been a huge part of my life and I've been an endurance athlete for most of it. Following the loss of Marty, though, I have been slow to get back to regular exercise. I'm still working on it. I understand that it is not unusual for the normal to disappear after a loss. Maybe more rigorous exercise is on the horizon for me.

Dance and yoga can be helpful ways to integrate the mind and body and get out of our heads. Others might find throwing pots, painting or sculpting. For me, collecting Pueblo pottery brings me into contact with the splendor of exquisite objects. Filling my life with beauty, living right beside a river, getting into nature, being with friends and family all feed my soul. Whatever does that for you, my friend, immerse yourself in it.

Poignant Journeys

After Marty had whole-brain radiation, started chemo, lost her hair, had operations on both hips and knew the cancer would take her, she wanted to travel to places that were important to her and to us as partners.

The first was to a sentimental favorite, Key West, Florida, where we had enjoyed great times together. On our second trip there, we were expecting warm, sunny beach days. Instead, we hit record cold weather. Marty was one big goosebump on that trip. Still, we went back several times, and it held great memories for us. On this last trip, Marty could still walk a little but to make it easier on her I pushed her in a wheelchair all over the island. We had a blast!

Another trip we took was to Moab, Utah where we spent time in Arches and Canyonlands National Parks. The parks had been among our favorite places to explore, take photographs and spend quiet time together. At this point, Marty had days when she felt okay and others that were not so easy. We drove around in our truck to see what we could see. At one point, we stopped and got the wheelchair out so I could push her along on a couple of dirt trails. We wanted to see some of the largest arches up close. When I was struggling with pushing the chair up a gradual incline, a kind soul appeared and helped us out. We met that kind of warmth and helpfulness many times.

We took another trip to Capitol Reef National Park, also in Utah. Marty was not feeling well this time, so we limited our sightseeing to a few hours a day and rested a lot. Still, she loved and enjoyed just being there. We ate in the room and watched movies when we weren't driving in the Park. Despite the limits, she was glad we went.

A bigger trip was a journey we took to Prescott, Arizona to

see her relatives. As I described this trip in Chapter 3, it was an arduous one for Marty. She was terribly ill by then, but she had this dream of seeing her family again even though they lived far away from us.

I shed wonderful, sentimental tears when I recall these outings. These are the kind of recollections that make me cry for missing her and smile at the joy we shared. Nothing can take those memories from us. Traveling to places that hold special meaning and seeing relatives for the final time can provide sustenance in the final months or weeks of life.

WRITTEN IN STONE

Gravestone art: Sounds morbid, right? I've spent quite a bit of time in our local cemetery, and I can tell you that gravestones are a way folks express what is important. There are hearts, airplane propellers, footballs, elk and deer, rivers, mountains, crosses and more.

Honoring Marty included, for me, the design of our gravestone. There are two endless knots on the stone. One knot stands for the constancy of existence and Marty's ongoing spirit. The other symbolizes the continued relationship Marty and I have, a relationship that transcends and cannot be defeated by death.

On the lighter side, engraved below an image of Buddha on the gravestone are two lotus flowers. An open lotus suggests enlightenment. Without really thinking through it, I had both lotus flowers engraved open. The one for Marty should, of course, be open. The other for me should, perhaps, have been engraved as only partially open! There is more about the gravestone that I will mention in the last chapter, but suffice it to say, gravestone art means a lot to me and also to many.

Going out to the cemetery to choose a gravesite was something

I dreaded. Can it get any sadder than that? A friend went with me for moral support, and that helped a lot. What changed everything about the experience was finding a single plot, just big enough for two cremation-size interments, situated between two ancient Cottonwood trees. The morning sun shines directly on the gravesite and is shaded midday by the trees. I find it a comforting place to come and talk, a peaceful spot where I can sit with my back up against a tree and spend time sharing with Marty about my life as well as thoughts, feelings and memories. Family and friends can come and do the same.

Although some of Marty's ashes are there, she's not "there" any more than she is confined to any physical place. Someday, our ashes—mine plus those of Marty's that are not interred at the site—will be together and placed in Taylor Reservoir, a clear, snow-fed, high mountain reservoir. The reservoir sends the Taylor River into a beautiful canyon, winding its way to become part of the Gunnison River, which then empties into the Colorado River. When any of our children or loved one visits any of those rivers, we will be there with them.

CHAPTER 18, COUNSELOR'S RESPONSE

In this chapter: Marv has shared with us how he journaled stories, drew pictures, participated in memorials, spent time with supportive family and friends, and purposefully traveled. He was intentionally accessing emotions related to his memories and doing so in ways that went beyond the benefit of spoken words. We know we are helped by opportunities to talk through our grief, but sometimes something more is needed.

Importance: We carry memories of our loved ones within our minds and bodies. We think of them as they endured illness, we hold on to images of what happened in an accident, we recall moments when we gave intimate care to them, and we remember details surrounding the event of their death.

Those of us who have experienced the loss of a loved one need to externalize painful emotions and give voice to internal messages. These inner responses can be expressed in images that represent a feeling or idea. A black cloud, for instance, can indicate sadness. Changes in the nature of these depictions—we can think of them as visual metaphors—can reflect changes in our viewpoint or behavior.

Clinical insights: When it comes to memories of a loved one's death, some level of trauma is internalized. The after-effects of trauma can be both psychological and physiological. The trauma of loss can lead to such symptoms as sleep disturbances, flashbacks, and memory impairment, as well as physical pain and addictions.

"Feelings of helplessness and hopelessness contribute to changes in self-image and contaminate interpersonal relationships. Emotional flooding and numbing, chaotic and conflicted thought processes, and maladaptive behaviors are symptoms that can be related to being overwhelmed by trauma."— B. Cohen, M. Barnes, A. Rankin, *Managing Traumatic Stress Through Art.*

What that suggests is that we need an outlet for internalized memories. Participation in the formation of art, as well as taking part in other physical activities, enables an outward expression of inward pain. "Traumatic memories exist in our minds and bodies in a state-specific form, meaning they hold the emotional, visual, physiological, and sensory experiences that were held at the time of the event…They're essentially undigested memories. Recovery … means working through these undigested memories until they no longer cause symptoms."—Erica Curtis, California-based therapist.

The usual treatments include talk therapy or cognitive behavioral therapy with the aim of desensitizing survivors by talking and expressing feelings about the event. But these therapies may not be enough. Art therapy provides an outlet when words fail. For example, to help clients identify coping strategies and internal strengths to begin the journey of healing, "they may create collages of images representing internal strengths."—Renee Fabian, *Healing Invisible Wounds: Art Therapy and PTSD*.

As adults we need to develop skills that allow us to overcome pain and stress and find ways to cope and continue living. "To overcome the impact of traumatic stress one needs to restore, or to develop, healthy ways to tolerate stress and pain, to have compassion and respect for oneself, to interact with others without compromising personal values and beliefs, and to make changes that allow for purpose and meaning in life."—B. Cohen, M. Barnes, A. Rankin, *Managing Traumatic Stress Through Art*.

Suggestions: It's often difficult to find the right words to express the complexities of loss. Consider an activity you're already familiar with or choose a new one you're willing to try, knowing that artistic ability is not necessary to gain the benefit of discovering images that will access your emotions. Many who choose writing, for example, find the 'nonjudgmental page' to be a healing place where they can freely record intimate or intrusive thoughts and make sense of those thoughts. The nonjudgmental page is also a place to release the recorded thoughts.

I always suggest getting help to process your memories, as

it can be overwhelming to do this work alone. A professional, licensed art therapist, familiar with grief, can provide guidance and ideas. If you're on your own, however, you can choose an art form or activity that feels suitable for you and spend regular, designated time working on it. You can express your feelings by forming a sculpture, creating artwork, writing poetry, scribbling or coloring, writing stories, creating a painting, building an object, planting a garden, cutting and gluing in a scrapbook, or memorializing a loved one through travel, to name some possibilities.

As you work, notice what emotions come up while you focus on the activity. Keep in mind that no matter what images emerge, they are your own and they are of great value. Do not dismiss them.

If you begin to experience a debilitating increase in anxiety or despair as you are working, refrain from the activity and seek guidance from a licensed professional. Because support plays a significant role in recovery and restoration, it is important to locate people who inspire your efforts to express yourself and include them or spend time with them as you work.

To carry the process even further, consider what changes in your thinking would contribute to shifting your emotions to a more positive or helpful frame of mind and incorporate those changes into your work or make another picture or item containing those changes. Focusing on what you'd most *like* to feel or think may point you towards the actual shift in emotions.

CHAPTER 19

———

A PRACTICAL PLAYBOOK FOR HELPING OTHERS WHO EXPERIENCE A LOSS

As one who grieves, I want to share some practical lessons I have learned from my experience. Whether you are suffering through a profound loss of a loved one or want to support someone who is mourning, there are effective and non-intrusive ways to help.

JUST LISTEN

I learned the value of listening when I was a practicing minister in the United Methodist Church. Between my experience at the Georgian Retirement Home during my graduate school years and the three-plus years I ministered at two local churches in Iowa, I conducted 130+ funerals. I had not anticipated that, nearly 50 years later, the time I spent helping families and friends through the grief process would scroll forward and help me in my own deep sadness.

What seems like a lifetime ago, I studied grief counseling at Garrett Graduate School of Theology, as it was known at the time. There we learned to give a person who is grieving the space to just BE and to say whatever is on their mind and heart, or not say anything. To express or not express whatever they are feeling at that moment is the best gift you can give.

As a practicing minister, I realized the importance of that training. I found that family members needed to talk about and be listened to when they brought up their memories, thoughts or feelings. Sometimes it was hard for me not to say something. I was tempted to interject my thoughts in order to make them feel better, fix them or break the silence. But my training helped me stay quiet. That was key.

When I was deep in the grief process myself, I wished people would just shut up and listen. Instead, what I often experienced was people being uncomfortable around me. Many seemed to think they had to say something to cut the silence or to fix how they thought I must be feeling. I think they often had to say something to help themselves feel better. That was why I didn't go to the grocery store in my small town for many months after Marty passed.

I have found that when I tried to talk about my feelings with my friends, some of them were good at listening, at just being there with me. Others, however well-meaning, felt impelled to say something that they thought would be comforting or, worse, profound. But bringing comfort to the grieving doesn't work that way. You cannot resolve someone else's sadness for them.

Here is another important point about listening: If a person speaking from their grief is interrupted, they are unlikely to get back to what they were saying or to the feelings they were having. When I was interrupted, I did not have the energy or concentration to return to the thoughts I had begun to express. The moment was fleeting. The opportunity for those feelings to be heard, understood and released was lost.

A person in grief has a brain that, to one extent or another, has been traumatized. I often lost my ability to track conversations and reconstruct what people were saying before I had been interrupted. People in their early days of grief may not have the energy to retrace their thoughts. I know I couldn't.

I also found that, if I was interrupted in expressing unresolved feelings, those feelings could possibly stick to me. This is important to keep in mind while you are quietly listening. Losing track of those feelings, it's as if I failed to listen to my own deeper wisdom that was embodied in the feelings I wanted to express. That wisdom is the same source that I hear in meditation. When I have sufficiently quieted my mind, I can sense what spiritual teacher Eckhart Tolle speaks of when he asks, "Who is it that is observing your thoughts?"

When I had sessions with Carol, she just listened when I needed to talk. She would provide her insights after I was done expressing myself. She and I have discussed how difficult it is for most of us to be quiet and listen, whether in grief or not. Many are simply uncomfortable with silence. Sitting or standing next to a grieving friend is an opportunity for you to get comfortable with silence and perhaps even with the impermanence of life.

LET THEM BE

A grieving person may express themselves through words, quiet tears, sobs or silence. Some folks simply cannot bear to hear the feelings. It's heartrending for them and I understand that. But the pain is real and needs space and time to express itself.

At my son Seth's house on the Thanksgiving following

Marty's passing, I cried at the Thanksgiving table. I was missing Marty so much. I couldn't help it and had no reason to suppress the tears. I was completely accepted at that table. I can remember Isabel, my wonderful daughter-in-law, reaching over and putting a hand on my shoulder without saying a word. My 3-year-old granddaughter asked me if I was okay. My family accepted my feelings, loved me, and once the moment was over, we went on to celebrate, give thanks and have a good time. Grief, when it is accepted as part of life, doesn't ruin events or times together, it enhances their authenticity.

BEING MORE THAN DOING

Caring for someone who has experienced a loss is more about being with them than doing something for them. We will get to what to 'do' for them later in the chapter. Perhaps one reason why helping someone who is grieving is difficult for us here in the US is that our culture and economy are built around taking action. We see a problem and respond with an action to fix it. I'm naturally built that way, too: See a problem, come up with a solution. Take action. Right away. No hesitation. That is no doubt part of the strength of our nation. We are solution-oriented.

I suggest hitting pause when it comes to helping someone who has experienced a loss. First, let's see what they are experiencing, what feelings and thoughts they are having. Second, let's listen and let them express what they need to express in the moments we are with them. Third, let's think about what to do or not do for them.

If the grieving person seems to want to talk, our job is to let them do that. If they are crying or quiet, we want them to feel they are not alone. If they are expressing anger or regrets, then we want them to feel they are heard, understood and accepted. All of these actions require us to pause, listen and, initially, not do anything other than be with them.

An Opportunity

Being there for a grieving person is an opportunity to get to know them when they most need to have someone around and when they most need to be known.

The first few months after Marty passed was the most vulnerable time of my life. My emotions were raw and exposed. I had few of the normal defenses to deal with issues or problems effectively and certainly not with other people's emotions. I was as empathetic for my children as I was able, but that is about all I could muster. The friends that were close to me during that time got to see my weaknesses, my strengths, my vulnerabilities, my sadness. Those people knew me before, but much more fully from being with me during the times of intense and continuous grief. Those friends that stayed with me during those days are my best and closest friends now.

I recently counted 19 friends with whom I can talk about anything. I realize how fortunate I am to be able to say that! I'm not sure who is more grateful—me for being helped, or them for being able to be helpful.

Being with someone who is grieving is an opportunity to get to know yourself better. You get a chance to listen to your own inner voice, to listen to your own thoughts as they come up in your mind. As you listen to their pain, it is a chance to listen to where your own sadness comes from, how it is affecting you today and how you feel it in your body. This is great information to help with your own healing and later as you experience losses. As I listened to grieving families during the course of my life, I was able to feel the unresolved pain from my own family of origin. That pain told me about my own unresolved losses. It was another opportunity for healing.

Suspend Judgment

When we truly love someone, I believe we suspend judgment. By that I don't mean we lose sight of what is really happening or deny reality. Suspending judgment means that we set our own issues aside and love the person as they are. We don't try to change them, correct them or fix them. This lesson came from Zen Master, Norma Wong, who taught me what it means to be present.

This is never more important than when we are with someone who is grieving. It is an opportunity to make the moments all about someone else, not about ourselves. Our culture sometimes encourages, even rewards, self-centeredness or even narcissism. But in these moments, folks who think it is all about them don't leave enough oxygen in the room for anyone else to breathe.

What Can We Actually DO for Someone Who is Grieving?

Carol writes about this extensively in her section of this chapter. But here are some pointers, based on my personal experience.

Reach out. Don't wait for them to call. They don't have the energy. You make the call.

Be present. Make yourself available. Hang out, but don't be a pest or a bother.

Be quiet. Nothing is about you in this situation.

Offer hope, not advice. There is a future. Be willing to be part of that future for this person whose days or years ahead may seem to have been taken away. One of the greatest things my son and others did was to help me think about what to do next. When he and I took that road trip together from Gunnison to Los Angeles, I couldn't think about the long-term future, but I could at least see the next week, the next step or two.

Give in tangible ways. That old tradition of bringing food by the house makes a positive difference. Who has the energy or the interest in cooking when your spouse or parent has passed away? I certainly didn't. Prepared food is welcome. Doing housework for a grieving family is physical relief for them when they are exhausted. Marty's half-sister arrived at the house and within an hour was cleaning the kitchen and vacuuming the floors. I felt supported and not alone.

Wash their car. Buy groceries. Run errands. Offer to make calls to friends. If there are kids in the household, create activities for them. Take younger kids to the park or older kids on a bike ride. Tangible things count and make a difference.

THE BUSINESS OF DEATH

One of the things most of us who experience the loss of a loved one face is what I refer to as the 'business of death.' There's a lot of work for survivors. I say work because the tasks are many and they are a drag when you least want to do this stuff.

If you want to support someone, help them with the business of death. After Marty passed, there were costs and paperwork for medical issues (doctor visits, hospital stays, lab work, chemo treatments, ambulance services, in-home caretaker) and death-related matters (coroner, undertaker, cemetery plot and gravestone, death certificates, head stone). Names on accounts had to be changed—on checking, savings and insurance; on investments, home mortgage and car loans; on credit cards and cable TV accounts. Because Marty and I were business partners, all the names on business accounts and companies needed to be changed, as well. There was catching up to do on all the personal business things I had set aside.

A really hard thing was to receive the death certificate. The local coroner was very helpful and printed a dozen because many organizations need a certificate to make changes in ownership to property, companies, insurance and the like. So, in the weeks and months following Marty's passing, I found myself corresponding with various folks and inserting a death certificate in the envelope. That was poignant and reminded me how my life had changed. In a way, these mailings helped me face reality.

Like so much of what I'm writing about in this book, it is hard to know what this is like unless you have experienced it yourself or helped someone else through it. The more integrated your life is with the loved one who passed, the more 'business of death' there will be to deal with. Likewise, the more complex your life together has been, the more business of death there will be as well. For Marty and me, it was extensive: four companies, real property, children and so much more. I'm pretty good when it comes to taking care of business, but this took me months—up to a year—to work through.

Children of elderly parents also deal with this when their parents pass. When my mother died at the age of 95, she was still paying her own bills and was sharp as a tack. She was, to put it candidly, full of piss and vinegar, and that memory makes me smile every day. Most responsible adults make the effort to have a Will or Trust to handle the financial aspects following death. Though my mother's estate was reasonably spelled out in a Trust, it took nearly a year and a half of dealing with lawyers and accountants in her home state of Iowa to get everything settled up. When we die, all of us leave behind the business of death—from death certificates and wills to phone and computer accounts to clothes, all of which are very, very personal.

After Marty passed, I could not tell whether managing all of the business of death was helpful to the grief process or it just kept the hurt coming. Or both. But the long and unavoidable slog simply had to get done. Some of the details are very painful. As I mentioned, helping someone with the business of death is a true gift.

WORK

Work can be a place where we take care of ourselves. Often, we have important and hopefully supportive relationships with work colleagues. The job itself can be a solace, a respite to focus on something other than the grief and loss. That is not all bad. Sometimes we just need to find some normalcy and work can provide that.

A warning, though: Work can just as easily be a place where we go to avoid facing our loss and grief. We may allow ourselves to be consumed by being busy, by activity that demands energy and attention. This way of 'staying busy' is one aspect of common wisdom and a part of how we often, in our culture, prescribe how someone should cope with grief. It goes something like, 'If you just stay busy, you'll be all right.' I still have people, five years later, who ask what I'm involved with and then add 'Ah, good, you're staying busy.'

Work is often necessary for economic reasons. My suggestion is to not let it demand so much of your time that you fail to be with yourself and your healing community. Work can wait at least a few days.

If you are a colleague, manager or business partner of a person who is grieving, you can give them a soft landing when they come back to work. This might mean offering them time off or part-time work for a while. You might have a team meeting among colleagues to plan for a quiet, thoughtful way to welcome them back to work or let them know how much you care about them. This may include attending the service for the loved one or sending flowers. One of our customers took a collection and sent hundreds of flowers for our deck while Marty was still alive. She loved it and it meant so much to both of us.

GET THEM TO THE HELP THEY NEED

In addition to the remarkable and caring support they gave Marty and me, our home health and hospice folks put us in touch with our counselor, Carol. As both she and I have said repeatedly, no one needs to go through a grief or loss crisis alone. You can help your friends, relatives and loved ones get the support they need when they need it. Don't hesitate or wait.

When a dear neighbor of mine was diagnosed with cancer, I immediately contacted Julie, the director at Living Journeys, and told her about my neighbor's illness. Julie shifted into high gear and got my neighbor the financial and logistical support she and her family needed, while she received treatments two hours away from home. Then when she returned home, Living Journeys delivered prepared meals to her door on a regular basis.

CHAPTER 19, COUNSELOR'S RESPONSE

In this chapter: Sharing our grief experiences with others—companioning—is an essential element in rebuilding our lives after the death of a loved one. Marv writes about how sharing can be accomplished for ourselves, as well as for another person who is grieving. The connectedness between people creates a collaborative process that has a restorative, healing power. This healing power is difficult for grieving individuals to achieve alone.

Importance: There has been an important shift away from our traditional views of grief as a solo experience. We now recognize that others play a *vital* role in the griever's discovery of his or her new and reconstructed life. Friends and relatives can play a key role in companioning a person in grief by being a good listener, a skill that takes practice. It involves quietly paying attention to another's words, or perhaps to their silence, and simply hearing them, without judgment and often with little to no comment—simply hearing them and remaining okay with what is said.

Clinical insights: Robert Neimeyer, a psychology professor at the University of Memphis, explained in his book, *Lessons of Loss: A Guide to Coping,* that grieving was once linked to a journey. A person entered the journey beginning at one place, moved through a desolate and unfamiliar terrain and then, with luck, returned to a place near their point of origin. The journey was a private and solitary one. Grief counselors functioned as travel consultants who suggested options to keep the person moving towards the journey's preordained end.

Today, according to Neimeyer's updated version of the experience, the grief journey is a boundless one "from which we will never completely return." He tells us that "this approach to mourning emphasizes the *joint role of others* in shaping the direction and pace of our journey, whether these others are members of our intimate circle of family and friends, or represent fellow travelers encountered along the way." In this version of the journey, the grief counselor "acts as a fellow traveler rather than consultant, sharing the uncertainties of the journey, and walking alongside, rather than leading the grieving individual along the unpredictable road toward a new adaptation."

Suggestions: Here are a few thoughts that will help with companioning. Much of the advice is adapted from the Hospice Volunteer Orientation manual, "Words of Advice for Bereavement Companioning."

Remain curious. Don't claim to be an expert.
Curiosity is more an attitude than it is about asking lots of questions. A client recently told me, "I wish people would NOT ask me questions, especially about what happened. It's hard to have to keep recalling details. I wish they would just comment on themselves." You could ask the person if they would LIKE to talk about their loved one. That gives them a choice.

Focus on learning from others. Don't teach them.
Don't claim expertise about someone else's grief. We can all learn from others about the ways they choose to express sadness. They deserve our respect for their individuality.

If you've ever had someone repeat a cliché to you or a well-worn phrase that sounds like advice, then you know how unhelpful and even demeaning that can feel. Don't repeat those phrases to your friend.

Walk alongside. Don't attempt to lead.
A companion is just that—someone who walks beside you. Remember this is *their* experience.

Discover the gifts of sacred silence. Don't fill a painful moment with words.
Most of us are uncomfortable with silence. Our tendency is to distract ourselves when confronted with it. However, it's powerful to remain still while experiencing the discomfort of pain.

Listen with your heart. Don't analyze.
Our scientific culture leans towards fact-based explanations. In the pain of grief, however, explanations do not always bring relief.

Be present to another's pain. Don't attempt to take it away.
Our culture has taught us that pain is bad and should be avoided. Within a grief experience we know that if we don't look at pain and recognize the validity to its existence, we can never adapt to its presence. Adapting to the very bitter and, somehow, "sweet" feelings that exist within grief is a major goal. We need to know we can exist with both the reality of our sadness and the will to continue living.

Respect disorder and confusion. Don't impose order and logic.
There should be no expectations for how another person will grieve. No question about this. Disorder is a logical result when someone's entire way of life has been assaulted because of a death. Respect their way of coping, and the chaos that exists until they find their balance.

Bear witness to the struggle. Don't try to direct it.
You are a witness, not a judge. Witnessing involves using eyes to observe, ears to listen, and sometimes arms to hug if the other person is open to it. Bearing witness means to stand with them and observe what is true for them. You are a fellow traveler.

Go to the wilderness of the soul with another human being. Don't feel responsible to "find a way out."

This is their journey, not yours. Many unknowns lie ahead. You can be present with someone without trying to fix their sadness, find solutions or explain the whys around their loss. Instead, buy groceries for them, bring them homemade muffins or go for a walk with them. Just don't try to find a solution to their pain.

CHAPTER 20

A LAST WORD FROM MARTY

Marty made the decision to be happy many times during her life and asked me to do the same. This I've written about in previous chapters. I've also noted that when she passed away, I had to learn how to rebuild my resiliency in order to move forward with life. I tapped into the core of Marty's life story and her way of enduring difficult times by turning to her inner spirit and strength.

I lived this aspect of Marty's approach to life during our time together. Our love and shared experiences built a reservoir of strength in each of us and in our relationship. We needed all of it when we faced cancer. Most especially, we needed the resolution to be happy. That determination not only built up our resiliency, but it was also there to help us through our desperate battle against a relentless illness and loss.

Despite these challenges, the decision to be happy created a sense of authentic optimism about our lives. We believed that nothing could defeat our love or our commitment to each other. We were right.

People who are optimistic tend to live longer (past 85 years), sleep better, are more consistent in their healthy habits and less likely to die from heart attacks, even when there is a family history of coronary events. These findings are from a 2019 study by the Harvard T.H. Chan School of Public Health that was conducted over a period of 25 years. The study's conclusion: Think positive, feel better, live longer!

What really amazed me, and what Marty taught me, was that we can literally make the decision to be happy. This is simple and very deep wisdom. Thank you again, Marty, for sharing this insight with me. Through Marty, I want to share with you the path we followed to being happy.

BE MINDFUL AND PRESENT IN THE MOMENT

Our fundamental decision to be happy grew out of our choice to be present, to enjoy and engage with every moment of the day. We believed that each day would bring love and even joy, no matter what else was happening. This is ultimately what got us through the battle with cancer.

Staying present in the moment at hand is invaluable in building resiliency into our lives. This is not always easy, since our brains produce a constant stream of thoughts and images. Focusing on what we are doing, thinking or feeling in the moment can train our lens on what's immediately important and produce the comfort of calm and the wisdom of insight.

Its value lies in its ability to stop us—to stop us for a few minutes from thinking, thinking, thinking. Its benefit is in the interruption of anxiety, fear or anticipation of the future or a negative focus on the past. This is invaluable during times of grief. Being mindful of our own thoughts and feelings gives us clarity, as well as respite from the intensity of the grief and emotions. By staying present we can give ourselves a break and possibly gain high-value insights along the way.

As you know from previous chapters, Marty was remarkably able to stay present under the most challenging circumstances. This is another message that Marty sends forward to us here and now.

LET GO OF WHAT HARMS YOU

As I've mentioned, I liked to kid Marty that she was born out of the belly of Buddha. That's because she had the ability to let go of the past if it was hurtful or harmful; she worried little about what may or may not happen in the future. This is an essential aspect of being present in the moment. I'm sure she had as many negative thoughts about the past or the future as anyone else. She just let them go and didn't spend time or energy on them. My sense was that this became a touchstone in her life when she was able to let go of the hurt related to her abuse as a young girl and make the decision not to live the life of a victim.

Interestingly, Marty was not very empathetic toward others, but was extraordinarily compassionate. Let me explain. When we first met, I was stunned at her exceptional level of compassion and how little energy she spent on empathy or sympathy. For her, sympathy in particular was demeaning toward the other person and disrespected their power to live their life as they saw fit. As to empathy, she did not think it was her role to try to feel what someone else was feeling. As to compassion, she trusted the feelings that arose within her when she saw the suffering of others and acted on those feelings.

She was an optimist about the human heart and believed that everyone is doing the best they can. This combination of compassion and belief in the goodness of people was her foundation. She trusted and believed in her own humanity and respected the same in others.

EMBRACE THE BEAUTY OF IMPERMANENCE

Most of us love life, love others and don't want any of it to end or even change. What Marty and I found was that the more we embraced the impermanence of life, the more we had a sense of urgency and the freedom to live every day as fully as possible. That certainly carried over into dealing with cancer and the subsequent decline in Marty's health.

Knowing and saying that we will all die is generally acknowledged. You know the saying—all we know for sure is death and taxes. The game changer is to embrace impermanence and let that give us more freedom to live life fully and in the ways we want to live it. John Brehm's wonderful compilation "The Poetry of Impermanence, Mindfulness, and Joy" brings this wisdom to us from over several centuries and cultures in a way that only poetry can. In the section on Mindfullness, Li Po (701-761), writes of watching a White Falcon.

Watching a White Falcon Set Loose

High in September's frontier winds, white
brocade feathers, the Mongol falcon flies

alone, a flake of snow, a hundred miles
some fleeting speck of autumn in its eyes.

Facing and embracing loss is an essential part of living a full life. In the early days of Marty's cancer diagnosis, we returned home from a lengthy stay at Penrose Hospital in Colorado Springs. We did our best to settle into the new reality. It was so good to be home again: the familiar views down our Valley, the smell of the Aspen and Pine in the fireplace, our log home, the feel of the wood floor under feet, our sweet golden retriever who could not stop licking Marty's face, and neighbors and friends who came by to offer support.

While it felt so good to be back in our home, it also brought queasiness to the pits of our stomachs. We had had so much wonderful support at Penrose Hospital, we really did not want to leave. I actually think they let us stay a couple of extra days because of how we were feeling. Back home, we once again had to face the inescapability of Marty's illness.

What to do now? We did in those early days what we had always done. We faced reality and moved forward. Marty was and still is a true teacher when it comes to living each day as fully as possible. One of the first things she did was to write the saying below on a peach-colored note card. She placed the card on top of the fireplace mantel, where it would always be in front of us. She told me, "This is how we will live."

Face Death
  At Any Moment
Live Life Fully
  At All Times
Learned at Chozen-Ji International Zen Dojo

It is often the small things that matter, that make life what it is. A friend once said that the small things are what make us human as we await our destiny. After Marty could no longer walk, she would come out for breakfast in the wheelchair and park in front of a window to take in one of her favorite views. I would ask her what her pleasure was for breakfast. Always coffee, sometimes orange juice and whatever sounded good to eat. She relished food when she was feeling well enough to eat. Ever watchful, she would share her observations of the birds, the deer or the clouds and deep blue Colorado skies. It all looked wonderful and beautiful to her. Earlier, I shared her joy with you when, one night we went out on the deck to see the starts and she declared, "This is the universe that will give me more life!"

In the beginning, when our oncologist Dr. Patel sat beside Marty's bed and, holding her hand, told us that Marty would die from the cancer, we were stunned and overwhelmed. As our minds gradually took that in, the losses or anticipated losses stacked up very quickly. Initially, we were staggered by the news and the reality of it.

I hope you will never experience anything like that. But if you do, just know that you are not alone. Many of us have and many more will face similar news. Living a life that continuously restores your own resiliency can get you through even something like a diagnosis of a deadly form of cancer.

Being ready to face death at any moment is living on the edge of awareness and truth. Living life fully at all times is deciding to be happy, to live and love with an open and vulnerable heart. To live a life full of meaning is a choice we make every day, every moment

Marty lived and died by the saying from the Dojo in Hawaii. She faced down the inevitability of the cancer taking her life, but at the same time she lived each day, each moment, as fully as she could. As a way of passing the Dojo's wisdom on to others, we had this saying engraved on our gravestone. It is also tattooed over my heart in her handwriting from the card on the mantel.

Our story, Marty's story, is one of great loss and great hope. The point of this part of our journey is not just that our death is inevitable. It is also that Marty was able to let go of life itself with a calm heart. She was not afraid. Why be afraid of something we don't know much about? And if we are not afraid of death, what is there to be afraid of?

Marty's message is that loss is inevitable. Life is not permanent. But every day we decide how we want to live.

A LAST WORD

The loved one you have lost would want you to move forward with your life and live it as fully as possible. I believe that and hope you do, too. Marty did everything, literally everything, that she could to gain another day of life. The least I can do is live with the same sense of urgency and gratitude.

Marty's message to us is simple: Live with an open heart. Love life. Love yourself and others with all your might.

Marty
It is too much to expect
A certain number of days here
Each one is the only
Opportunity

Only today exists
This moment, breathe,
Warmed by the sun
Guided by your foot prints

ACKNOWLEDGMENTS

With deep gratitude, we want to thank our families, colleagues and friends who have encouraged us to write this book. At times, it has been an emotional journey to retell the stories and reflect on those experiences. Carol and Marv have been the recipients of grace, understanding, and encouragement to continue and to finish this work.

We are grateful beyond words for the relentless support, encouragement and guidance from our publisher, Jon Finkel and Ballast Books. Thanks to Jon, our story is now accessible to all those who have lost loved ones and those who support them.

We would like to acknowledge our editor, Penny Lemov, for her wisdom, rapid responses and outstanding editorial contributions. She shares much credit for the quality of the manuscript.

We acknowledge all of the marvelous authors who have gone before us. You have taught us so much. Though we have acknowledged your work in the Bibliography, we want to thank you and encourage you to keep writing about this essential human experience.

Lastly, we want to acknowledge all of our fellow humans who have lost loved ones. You are our teachers. Your tears are our tears. Your hopes are our hopes.

Reading List

Bibliography of reading material and websites cited in the book or suggested as additional reference.

Books and articles:

American Psychiatric Association. *The Diagnostic and Statistical Manual of Mental Disorders (DSM-5)* E-Book

Brehm, John. *The Poetry of Impermanence, Mindfulness, and Joy.*

Brehm, John. *The Dharma of Poetry.*

Brown, Byron. *Soul Without Shame: A Guide to Liberating Yourself from the Judge Within*

Chast, Roz. Can't We Talk About Something More Pleasant?

Chethik, Neil. *FatherLoss: How Sons of All Ages Come to Terms with the Deaths of Their Dads.*

Chozen Ji International Zen Dojo of Hawaii: "Face Death at Any Moment, Live Life Fully at All Times."

Cohen, B., Barnes, M., Rankin, A. *Managing Traumatic Stress Through Art: Drawing from the Center.*

Collet, Teri. "Making the Most of Every Moment, A Patient's Guide to Living with Hospice." Booklet from Limbertwig Press.

Collins, Billy. "Shoveling Snow with Buddha". *The Poetry of Impermanence, Mindfulness, and Joy* edited by John Brehm. online at <u>American Poems.com</u>

Devine, Megan. *It's OK That You're Not OK: Meeting Grief and Loss in a Culture That Doesn't Understand*

Doughty, E.A., Wissel, A., & Glorfield, C. (2011). "Current Trends in Grief Counseling", <u>http://counselingoutfitters.com/vistas/vistas11/Article_94</u>

Dryden, Windy. "Regret can seriously damage your mental health—here's how to leave it behind." <u>The Guardian</u>

Fabian, Renee. "Healing Invisible Wounds: Art Therapy and PTSD." <u>Healthline.com</u> Farber, Stuart and others. Issues in End-ofLife Care, Family Practice Faculty Perceptions (July 1999 issue of Journal of Family Practice)

Frankl, Viktor E. *Man's Search for Meaning*

Gibran, Kahlil. *The Prophet*.

Golden,Thomas. *Swallowed by a Snake: The Gift of the Masculine Side of Healing*.

Hamlet, Melanie, "Men have No Friends and Women Bear the Burden," Harpers' Bazaar.

Hannig, Anita. "Talking About Death in America: An Anthropologist's View." <u>Undark.com</u>. <u>https://undark.org/2017/10/19/death-dying-america-anthropologist/</u>

Hendricks, Mark, *How to Use Grief Dosing to Get Through the Day*.

Jacobs, Selby. *Traumatic Grief: Diagnosis, Treatment, and Prevention*

Klass, Dennis, Walter, Tony, "Processes of Grieving: How Bonds are Continued"

Klass, Silverman & Nickman, *Continuing Bonds: New Understandings of* Grief

Neff, Miriam. *From One Widow to Another: Conversations on the New You.*

Neimeyer, Robert. *Lessons of Loss: A Guide to Coping*

O'Connor, Mary-Frances et al. "Functional Neuroanatomy of Grief: An fMRI Study." Amer. J. of Psychiatry 2003 researchgate.net

Parkes, Colin Murray. *Bereavement: Studies of Grief in Adult Life*

Pfeiffer, Richard. *Real Solution Anger Management Workbook.*

Schupp, Linda. *Grief: Normal, Complicated, Traumatic.*

Sojun, Ikkyu. Poems in John Brehm. The Poetry of Imperma nence, Mindfulness, and Joy

Stroebe, Hansen, Stroebe & Schut, *Handbook of Bereavement Research: Consequences, Coping and Care,* American Psychological Association

Tatkin, Stan. *Wired for Love: How Understanding Your Partner's Brain and Attachment Style Can Help You Defuse Conflict and Build a Secure Relationship*

Tolle, Eckhart. *The Power of Now: A Guide to Spiritual Enlightenment*

Tolle, Eckhardt. *A New Earth*

Wortman, C.B. and Silver, R. C., "The Myths of Coping with Loss Revisited"

Williams, Mary Beth and Poijula,Soili. *The PTSD Workbook*

Wolfelt, Alan. *Understanding Your Grief: Ten Essential Touch-stones for Finding Hope and Healing Your Heart*

Zucker, Robert. *The Journey Through Grief and Loss: Helping Yourself and Your Child When Grief Is Shared*

Websites

American Cancer Society, Coping With the Loss of a Loved One. https://www.cancer.org/treatment/end-of-life-care/grief-and-loss.html

American Dance Therapy Association. https://www.adta.org/

Chua, Celestine. "How to Find Your Life Purpose." Personal excellence https://personalexcellence.co/topics/

Hospice Website https://hospicefoundation.org/Volunteer

Psychology Today We Need to Talk About Death | Psychology Today https://www.psychologytoday.com/us/blog/handy-hints-humans/201703/we-need-talk-about-death

Psychology Today. Art Therapy https://www.psychologytoday.com/us/therapy-types/art-therapy

T.H. Chan School of Public Health, Harvard University https://www.hsph.harvard.edu/news/features/new-evidence-that-optimists-live-longer/

VeryWellMind. How Listening to Music Can Have Psychological Benefits. https://www.verywellmind.com/surprising-psychological-benefits-of-music-4126866